D1395269

KIND
WORDS
FOR
UNKIND
DAYS

Also by Jayne Hardy

The Self-Care Project
365 Days of Self-Care
Making Space

KIND
WORDS
FOR
UNKIND
DAYS

Everyday wisdom to help you
feel calmer and happier

JAYNE HARDY

First published in Great Britain in 2020 by Orion Spring
an imprint of The Orion Publishing Group Ltd
Carmelite House, 50 Victoria Embankment
London EC4Y 0DZ

An Hachette UK Company

5 7 9 10 8 6 4

A CIP catalogue record for this book is
available from the British Library.
ISBN (Hardback) 978 1 3987 0050 5
ISBN (eBook) 978 1 3987 0051 2
Printed and bound in Great Britain by Clays Ltd, Elcograf S.p.A.

ORION
SPRING

www.orionbooks.co.uk

For Peggy – the kindest person I know

Contents

Introduction

We're all going to experience unkind days; that's a surety. The kind words on those days? They're not such a given. For many (not always sensical) reasons, we tend to shoulder the unkind days: to muddle through, scared to unburden ourselves. As a result, we close ourselves up to allowing the channels of kindness to flow. All the while there's a broken record of unhelpful, internal, not-so-kind thoughts playing away.

Not only may we be partial to a bit of self-unkindness, but it's also easy to time-travel back to when someone has said something unkind to us. When they've, in no uncertain terms, expressed their disdain for our decisions, choices and behaviours. Those words leave their mark. On a rational level we know that says more about what they're going through than us, but it smarts all the same.

In a world that's so hot on the more assertive attitudes,

such as tenacity, go-get-'ems and hustle, kindness can get overlooked. Yet it's kindness that has the power to soothe, calm, ground, balance and restore. It's the balm of kindness that can ease the most troubled of times. It's kindness that, when in short supply, we hanker after with thirst. Kindness transforms, it encourages and it connects humanity. It's the possibility that's whispered in among the kind words. It's the straightening of a back, the beaming smile, the shimmer of self-belief – all fostered by a kind word or two. It's contagious too, this being kind. It sends ripples through our encounters and motivates and inspires through generations. For kindness is not only transformational; it's magic.

The other thing about kindness is that within its gentleness is a ferocity that can last a lifetime. We can all remember a time we were on the receiving end of kind words or a kind gesture and it sticks with us, continuing to provide warmth and comfort as the years roll by. That knowing nod is validating, uniting and provides a respite from the oftentimes tortuous internal dialogue. The more we have a flow of giving and receiving kindness, the more our hearts feel open to what the world has to offer.

This book is full of kind words for your unkind days. The kind words have been grouped together so that depending on how the day is being unkind to you, or, as is sometimes the case, how you may be being unkind to yourself, there is something for you no matter the situation. Read cover to cover, dip in at random or be a little more strategic, whatever works for you. Also feel free to take photos of any of the pull-out quotes that resonate with you and use them as your phone wallpaper or print them for your wall. This book is for you.

In trying to encapsulate my hopes for how this book might make you feel, I've written this poem:

I'll Sit With You in the Darkness

I'll sit with you in the darkness
I'll hope and I'll stay
For you mightn't know it yet
But life has more than this for you
On the other side of this
There's a life you won't want to miss
Until you see a glimmer of what I see in you
I'll sit with you in the darkness
There'll be head pats and kind words
A whisper of your magic
And a future that's yours to hold
I'll sit with you in the darkness
When the foggy clouds have lifted
I'll hold your hand and smile
It might have taken a while, but I was never in doubt
That we'd get you through the darkness

Because I've been to some of the darkest places in my mind, I understand how lonely such places can be and how painful the anguish. This book is full of kind words born from my own experiences or from words I often need to hear.

Sending love aplenty,
Jayne

Kindness
is not only
transformational;
it's magic.

1

Words for the days that feel frightening

The words within this chapter will be especially helpful to you if you are feeling scared, nervous and afraid. They'll calm your racing heart and help you to recognise your might.

We're all winging it

Nobody knows what the future holds. Nobody has all their ducks in a row. Nobody has a life free from problems, regrets, disagreements or stumbles. Nobody has all the answers.

There isn't anybody who isn't winging it.

And yet we're terribly frightened of getting things wrong. Even though we all get things wrong.

We avoid doing something that's different because we don't want to muck it up. Even though mucking up is part of the learning process.

Standing up and speaking out scares us because we fear judgement and criticism. Even though we're judged if we do and judged if we don't.

We don't ask the questions we want the answers to because we don't like to feel stupid. Even though nobody knows everything. We all start somewhere.

Being our true selves opens us up to rejection. Even though we can't be everyone's cup of tea, whoever we are.

Maintaining our 'yup, I'm calm and collected' masks because we don't want to look incapable. Even though we're all juggling balls as best as we can.

We're all winging it. We're all navigating a path that is ridden with obstacles and uncertainty – without a map to guide us. We're all feeling vulnerable.

Let's embrace the winging-it way. Let's be more open about the pickles we find ourselves in. Let's be generous about the discombobulation. Let's forgo the edited highlights and hustle, and open-arm the realness.

Don't believe the fearful thoughts

Friend or foe, how we feel about fear very much depends on how much of a hold it has on our day-to-day life.

Fear is normal. It pops its head up to make sure we're prepared for any perceived threats that might step daily into our paths. It doesn't check once, or twice, but keeps on keeping on until we act, or don't.

It can also pop up in the most ordinary of times, times when we're chilling, and suddenly fear will arrive saying, 'Oh, hello, you don't want to rest on those laurels of yours, do you? Have you thought about [this scary thing] lately?' It can turn the seemingly normal into something that strikes terror. It can do a one-eighty on our feelings about something we've done a trillion times before. It can be a friend when there's a lion battering down the garden gate, but it can also be a foe when it plays tricks on our mind. And it can spout nonsensical tirades with its but . . . but . . . buts.

There are times when it tells the biggest and cruellest of lies. It tells us that we won't get through this. We don't have what it takes. We're not strong nor brave enough.

Awful, awful lies. At a time when kindness and patience

and love is what we need, our brains make a self-doubt soup that makes everything all the harder for us.

If you're going through a particularly atrocious time of it, please don't believe fear when it diminishes who you are and who you could be. It plays dirty; it pulls out every wobble, every insecurity, every hurt, and it totally forgets the plenitude of times it's done that already and you proved it wrong.

If fear is holding you back from making a step towards a dream, from putting yourself forward for a job or from feeling worthy of making an appointment, then look it square in the eye and sod it – you've got this.

You can, and you will, get through this. You absolutely do have what it takes. You are strong and brave. You are deserving of all the wonderfulness there is.

Fear underestimates you

Fear underestimates your tenacity, your resilience. It forgets to remind you of all the times you've had to overcome it and all the times you've been triumphant. It casts aside your power, your heart and your capacity to see past whatever it is, to the other side where you're doing cartwheels of pride. It forgets that there are no mammoths chasing us across the plains, that life has evolved, even if its response to stuff hasn't.

Fear tries to deny us the potential freedom, joy, opportunity and love that could be beyond the hurdle. It taunts us with all that could go wrong, without showing us how it might go so right. It sentences us to doom and it diminishes us by interrupting our sleep, serving a dollop of self-doubt and injecting the most bizarre scenarios into our imaginations. And it completely and utterly underestimates you.

Whatever pesky shenanigans fear is playing right now, don't let it lower your expectations of your capacity to overcome it, because you are mighty, even when you don't feel it – *especially* when you don't feel it.

You deserve a bravery medal

When we think of bravery, we don't always think it applies to us.

After all, we haven't fought a tiger recently. We probably haven't rescued anyone from a burning building. We might not have made it out of bed.

But hold your horses a moment – those things aren't the only way bravery manifests itself.

A dictionary definition of 'bravery' is this:

bravery
/ bre v( )ri/
noun

Courageous behaviour or character.
'Perhaps I'll get a medal for bravery.'
Great bravery.
'They fought with exemplary heroism.'

Synonyms:
braveness, courage, courageousness, valour, valiance,
intrepidity, intrepidness, boldness, daring, audacity,

audaciousness, fearlessness, doughtiness, dauntlessness, pluck, indomitability, stout-heartedness, lionheartedness; backbone, spine, spirit, fortitude, mettle, gallantry, chivalry, grit, spunk, gutsiness, ballsiness[*]

It takes grit to keep showing up, to keep trying again and again. To battle through the pain, the frustration, the numbness and the uncharted territory that life brings. After all, we're not even taught what bravery is at school, never mind how to handle it.

It's quite probable that you have even saved a life – yours. Because, let's not make any bones about it, tough times can take lives.

And for those of us who feel ready to talk about our experiences and to tackle the societal stigma that doesn't seem to be going away anytime soon, we'll never truly understand the impact that talking about tough times might have on someone who's listening. Someone who's grateful that you're saying the words they're struggling to find. Grateful for the knowing nod signalling they're not alone. That's gallantry, right there.

[*] See 'Heroism' and 'Bravery', www.lexico.com/definition and www.lexico.com/synonym (accessed 03/08/20)

It takes grit to
keep showing up,
to keep trying
again and again.

You're braver than you think

We don't *feel* brave, though, do we?

We feel as though we're lacking in some way. Lacking in support? Probably. Sadly. Lacking character? Not on your nelly.

When those cruel thoughts tell you that you're not brave, reread this page over and over and over again, because there's so much evidence to the contrary. You might be scared, you might feel wary, you might well be resting, but you're a soldier. There's absolutely no doubt about that.

And if you do doubt it (because, you know, you're a humble so-and-so . . .), here's a dictionary's definition of 'to soldier on':

informal
Carry on doggedly; persevere.
'Graham wasn't enjoying this, but he soldiered on.'

Synonyms:
persevere, persist, carry on doggedly, keep on, keep going, not give up, struggle on, hammer away, be persistent, be determined, see/follow something through, keep at it, show determination, press on/ahead, stay with something, not take no for an answer, be tenacious, be

pertinacious, stand one's ground, stand fast/firm, hold on, hold out, go the distance, stay the course, plod on, plough on, grind away[*]

* See 'Soldier On', www.lexico.com/definition and www.lexico.com/synonym (accessed 03/08/20)

2

Words for the days that feel overwhelming

If you're after some calm, reassuring and encouraging words because life is getting too much and you feel ill-equipped to handle it, then you've landed in the right place.

You'll get to it

About that floordrobe. Do you have one?

You *could* feel ashamed. You *could* also lament your laziness. You *could* use it to berate and punish yourself.

But instead? Try seeing it for what it is: a physical representation of what's going on for you mentally.

When we're mentally firing on all cylinders (rare, but it's been known to happen), we don't have a floordrobe, nor do we have piles of post to open, a list of cancelled plans, grubby hair, disorganised paperwork, an overflowing inbox, an empty fuel tank.

It sometimes takes us a while to catch up with what these physical manifestations are indicating, but we get there.

They typically illustrate that we might be overwhelmed, lacking in energy and motivation, have bitten off more than we can chew, are struggling with anxiety, self-doubt and unworthiness, or that we might be unwell. They depict the messiness of our thoughts, the foggy head, the I'm-a-bit-done-in-ness.

They signal the need to stop. And here's the important bit: to stop and *not* beat ourselves up about stopping, to *not* compare ourselves to those who we think wouldn't ever have a floordrobe in the first place and to *not* put pressure on ourselves to get our ducks back into the straightest of rows. Just the need to stop and take stock.

And when we do that, clarity comes a-knocking. We've probably been feeling pretty squiffy for a while. It's possible that our boundaries have gone a bit wonky again. It's very likely that self-care has gone awry. It's incredible that we've kept on keeping on.

Whatever it is that you need right at this moment in time, get it. Prioritise it, make room for it, tell other people about it. It's the very least that you deserve.

That floordrobe? You'll get to it. But first? Get to you.

Nobody has perfection down pat

Just as we lament external mess, we also resent our internal mess. We see it as a sign that we're not whole, that we're broken, that we're flailing.

But in order for things to slot into place, they're often messy until they're not.

Consider your handwriting when you were learning how to write. It'd be larger than life, you'd forget where the joins were meant to be, there'd be big black lines through the mistakes and yet . . .

You kept at it. You tried and tried and tried again until it became second nature. You can now write on autopilot and what once *felt* messy no longer does.

This can be applied to everything you've ever learned. It was messy until it wasn't. There's a reason we needed a driving instructor to guide us towards and through our driving test; we'd be unsafe behind that wheel otherwise.

Learning to walk is fraught with knocks and scrapes. *Until it's not.*

Learning to talk is rife with mumbles and random sounds. *Until it's not.*

Learning to read is a scramble of words. *Until it's not.*

Learning is clumsy, obstacle-heavy, laden with all the lessons of how we're doing it wrong. *Until we're not.*

We don't often allow ourselves that grace and space to be a 'learner' despite the fact that anything we do that's new, different or challenging is a learning experience where we're the beginner who is embarking on a series of slip-ups, falling into place-ness and rinse and repeat. *Until we're not.*

The thing about this mess is that we don't half give ourselves a bad time about something that's unreservedly normal. In fact, it's all we've ever known as we've learned to crawl, walk, talk, write or do anything that we didn't previously know how to do. We're born adept at working through the mess, but as we grow older we also become well versed in that unfriendly and stifling component called perfectionism.

If you're in the middle of an internal mess right now, take the next step. Keep trying. Keep reminding yourself that you were born with an innate ability to take chaos and make sense of it. Don't let your fear of being imperfect hold you back – it didn't always and it doesn't have to now.

Don't worry about winning the day – go smaller

We're encouraged to think big, tear down those self-limiting beliefs and to stop being blind to the possibilities that surround us. Those things all *absolutely* have a place once we're rocking and rolling with health.

Arguably, though, if that's the macro, then we also have to make room for the micro, because that's the underlying success story in all the groundbreaking, award-winning, crushing-it tales. It is the things we do repeatedly day in and day out that form the fundamental basis for the macro stuff that's built upon it. The micro is the unsung hero.

Let's be clear, we're not even thinking about winning the day; it's even more micro than that – it's winning the minutes. Despite what's going on, doesn't winning a minute feel suddenly so much more manageable as we fling back our shoulders and take a deep breath? Sixty seconds versus you. Bets are on you – always, no matter what.

In the same way that we're taught to look after the pennies because the pounds will look after themselves, if we look after the minutes, then the days and weeks and months and years will look after themselves.

Looking after the minutes slows us down momentarily. It forces us to be present (a very good thing) and it demands that we listen to what we need in that exact moment (an extraordinarily very good thing) and in doing so we're much more likely to deliver whatever it is we need to ensure we feel victorious in that minute. Creating micro-systems and micro-moments to tune in and realign helps the minutes to stack up in a more conscious way.

It sounds far too simple but give it a go. Sit still and listen to yourself – what do you need? A drink, a pee, some silence, some white noise, more sleep, to stretch your legs, to brain-dump, to make a list, to cancel a prior engagement, to make an appointment to speak to someone . . .? What's disturbing your inner sanctuary right at this moment? What's making you feel 'off'? What action can you take, without delay, to realign?

You're a human 'being'

We don't always find it easy to squeeze time for the 'being' part of adulthood. It's all about the 'doing'; the responsibilities, the life admin, the adulting. We promise ourselves that when our to-do lists are completely crossed off, we can kick back and relax. Then, and only then, will we be able to relish in the stillness, totally guilt free.

But that time never comes because life is an escalator, a conveyor belt of this and that, constantly shouting for our attention.

We could literally do, do, do all day, every day, and still not feel as though we're on top of things because 'things' crop up willy-nilly. And we're proper brilliant at giving those things our attention, so much so that we divert all our attention to those things and wonder why on earth we feel so done-in.

In our quest to get everything completed, we've stopped hearing how we feel and what we need, we've become a spluttering metaphorical energy tank that's running on dredges. We're living in a never-ending episode of *The Generation Game*, on a loop. We're sat on that conveyor belt, whirring around and around.

But we can press pause. We can. Really.

Stopping doesn't change our worth; we're worthy whether we're doing or not doing. The people who feel we're not worthy when we stop, aren't worthy of our attention, love and energy.

Pressing pause gives us that breather, that breath, that space to hear and heed what's going on for us before we're forced to stop, because nobody can keep on keeping on without a maintenance break.

And if it helps, think of it like that: taking a break is similar to when we take our cars in for their MOT; to identify wear and tear, to look for the bits that might need some love and care; to give those things love and care so that everything is ready to set off again. We MOT our cars on clockwork, so it makes sense then that we should have a regular MOT slot for ourselves.

You don't just deserve a break, you *need* one, guilt free. Those other things can wait, they always can, but our health? Not so much. That's the golden stuff that we want to take care of, prioritise and protect.

We can
press pause.
We can.
Really.

There is no time machine

Time is a wily ol' beast because it'll pass no matter how we choose to spend it. It often feels as though it slips through our fingers and we try to mitigate that by planning back-to-back stuff to do – with no breathing space in between. We jump from one thing to the next to the next to the next to the next. In among the go-go-go we often find that we're saying no-no-no to ourselves and to what actually, really, matters to us.

Another odd thing about time is that we never really know, in the grand scheme of things, how much of it we're given in our lifetime. We put off the joyful, happy-soul connections and stillness to 'later'. 'Later' being that mirage of time that we never quite get to with all the noise and hustle and bustle that filters in and makes the fun stuff seem like pie in the sky. For another day, for another time. Frivolous, not deserving of, not worthy enough of, not now.

Sadly, there is no crystal ball that allows us to see how our future might play out or how much of that 'later' time we have left. Thankfully, though, we have more choices than we might imagine. We have more say over how we spend our time than it first seems. And, by golly, we all deserve the light to the dark, laughter to the tears, the space to the clutter and to do the things that make our hearts go a-flutter.

Yes, that totally and utterly includes you.

What one thing, that's for YOU, are you procrastinating about or pushing aside? What experience, connection, restorative thing have you put off and off and off and off, so much so that you've given up on it a bit? It's the thing that evokes longing, gives you butterflies of excitement; maybe it feels like it belongs to a different you – a not so lemoned-by-life you, or possibly you just think that ship has sailed. Perhaps it's a career, a goal or an adventure. Maybe it's less doing and more space.

Assess what, why, how and when? What would we like to be doing instead? Why do we keep saying 'yes' to every sodding thing else? How can we renegotiate how we're spending our time? And when are we going to start giving ourselves the very best of ourselves? Health and happiness is something we all deserve. All of us. No buts about it.

You are the boss of you

When our lives are filled with obligations, responsibilities and to-do lists, overwhelm can set in. That overwhelm can bring with it a feeling of loss of control.

The shoulds – they weigh heavy. The deadlines – they loom large. The expectations – they press and they press hard.

In all of this we'd be forgiven for forgetting who's boss. We'd be forgiven for thinking that we're answerable to all and sundry. We'd be forgiven for mistaking who is at the reins.

It boils down to you. *You* are the boss of you, now and always. And that's easy to forget in a world where people set limits, express themselves so very clearly and loudly, and want us to do and behave as they do and behave.

The world we live in, though, has been socially constructed. Which means you can pretty much deconstruct most of what's not serving you.

We're in charge of our own lives. The paths we lead don't have to be so convoluted and polluted. We're each entirely responsible for ourselves once we hit that grand ol' ripe age of adulthood.

When everything feels out of control we can choose to

take charge. To empower ourselves to say 'stop!' To get off the bandwagon. To redress, to remedy and to readjust to who we are and who we want to be. To renegotiate, renew and to reconnect to what it is that matters to us.

You are absolutely and incontestably the boss of you.

Switch it all off

We live in an information-rich time. There's an endless amount of topics we can search for on Google. There's unsolicited advice and sought-after advice coming in at all angles. There are opinions, expectations, alerts, notifications, apps, perspectives and oh-so much more, which flood our senses and our headspace with everything that's outside of us.

And we wonder why we feel lost in who we are and what we want and what we like and what we don't like.

We lament our minds for flooding with thoughts as soon as our minds hit the pillow.

We get frustrated by our seeming indecision and inability to focus.

We carry the burden of ways we might have disappointed others by not matching up to their expectations of us.

It's all noise, and it comes from the outside in. It drowns out our own wishes and wants. It knuckles our self-esteem and our self-worth. It makes us lose sight of the individuality of who we are. It takes our unique blend of colours of the rainbow and leaves us feeling beige.

In order to switch back into who we are, we need to learn to switch off all that external chatter.

We can do this by creating moments of quietude throughout the day, by leaning into spells of silence, by turning off alerts and notifications, by actively looking for the stillness that naturally existed in a pre-smartphone era, by exploring how *we* feel about things as opposed to how we're told to feel.

Because of all the things we deserve the most it's the comfort, ease, authenticity and conviction to be who we are and who we want to be. And to figure that out means spending time with our wildest aspirations and inspirations in an uproarious and rollicking way.

Don't be afraid to pop the outside world on hold while you plug into the wisdom you already hold inside.

3

Words for the days when you don't feel as though you matter

If it's one of those unkind days that leaves you feeling small and in need of championing and some gentle pep talks, look no further than the words within this chapter.

You *are* important

There are times when, try as we might, our brain feels like the cogs are coated in treacle. Every task, every thought, feels bogged down in weightedness and belatedness.

As if life isn't challenging enough, the foggy thoughts and boggy brain make everyday life feel like a gargantuan mountain to climb and the fatigue swashbuckles us from every direction possible. For anyone who has ever known the darkness of mental ill health or grief, they'll understand how incredibly impossible it can feel to brush their teeth – something we do, when well, on autopilot every single day without thought, without it using up all our spoons, without it feeling like such an overwhelmingly intimidating task.

Typically we take this personally, as a sign that we can't hack the pace, that we're not up to scratch, that we could or should do and be better.

What we don't account for is the sustained periods of time where we've given 110 per cent. Those times when we've dug to the deepest of depths to keep on truckin' on and swallowed feelings of unease to explore at a later date because when they popped up it wasn't the 'right' time. We forget the instances we flaked on our plans to rest up and we forget that we've demanded so much of ourselves along the way. We forget that we're not machines. *We forget how important we are.*

Self-care at its essence asks us to make choices mindfully based on weighing up where we are right now and where we'd like to be. It sounds so simple, so easy, so doable. It's doable, but it's far from easy.

When thinking is akin to walking in treacle and brushing our teeth feels ridiculously hard, we've just got to the stage where we've had enough. *More* than enough. It's our brain's way of saying 'hold up, you might want to keep on ploughing ahead, but I need a break and I'm going to darned well take one. Now.' Heed that.

Nurture the cues from your physical being that you're overdue a break:

Factor in breaks.
Factor in sleep.
Factor in talking to supportive people.
Factor in your needs.
Factor in handing over some of the 'doing'.
Factor in space to investigate how you feel.
Factor in the chance to explore those beautiful dreams
of yours.
Factor in the tweaking, pivoting and flexing.
Factor in time that's yours, a non-cancellable you-date.

And when the brain gets boggy please stop, or at the very least take your foot off the accelerator.

You are worth so much more than anything that is due, overdue, nagged of you or demanded of you. So much more.

You're allowed to take up space

The truly torrid times have us hidden in the shadows. They follow us to the sun and the fun. They're the sapper of joy and thief of energy. They bring with them hard-to-handle thoughts that can be incessant and unnecessarily evil.

Thoughts that tell us we're oversharers, snowflakes, that nobody gives a damn.

Thoughts of how we're burdensome, that we need to change this and that to be acceptable and accepted.

Thoughts on top of our thoughts on top of our thoughts.

Thoughts with no magic 'decrease volume' or 'mute' button. (Oh, how we'd love one of those!)

Thoughts that run on a wild rampage, which take all our mental energy to reason with, ignore or carry on regardless.

These thoughts are diminishing in their nature, and without support, without a shoulder to lean on, without people to challenge any skewed perspectives, those thoughts really affect our actions too.

We become afraid to take up space.

We don't call to make that doctor's appointment.
We apologise when other people knock into us.
We're apologetic for just being.
We're apologetic in every which way.
We don't assert our boundaries.
We stoop our shoulders.
We do everything we can to not stand out.
We change our minds about plans but don't change the
*   plans for fear of being a nuisance.*
We bend, twist and compromise to accommodate others.
We don't use the telephone helplines because we don't feel
*   worthy, even when in crisis.*
We don't allow ourselves to shine.

You absolutely are worthy of the appointments and care that's there.

If someone bumps into you, that's on them.

You are allowed to take up space and to make space for yourself.

You are allowed to be who you want to be.

Don't apologise for who and how you are. Those boundaries of yours, they're important and vital for good health.

Take a deep breath and stand tall.

You will always stand out because you're unique in the best possible way.

You're absolutely allowed to change your mind.

Please don't compromise yourself to keep others happy.

Use the telephone helplines when in crisis.

Allow yourself to shine as you are.

You, as you are right now, are bloomin' brilliant. You're full of miracles and magic, kindness and light, laughter and love. Elbow those imposter thoughts out of the way (don't be afraid to ask for help with this) and let a little more of you through. Take the floor, take the mic, take the space, it's your time.

You're full of miracles and magic, kindness and light, laughter and love. Elbow those imposter thoughts out of the way and let a little more of you through.

There's a power in you

Mightiness doesn't always roar. It's not always the flexing of muscle, the rumble of thunder, the bellows that we hear when we see sportspeople in action.

It can be the silent intake of a breath. The whisper of hope. The holding of hands. The mental tussle. The gentle pat on the back.

You're mighty. Even when you don't feel it, you're mighty. The strength you possess that gets you through those tough days – that's mightiness. That bounce-back-ability that sees you getting back up after falling down over and over – that's mightiness. Those actions you take that give hope its backbone – that's mightiness too. The holding on, not giving up, asking for help – it's all mightiness. All of it.

Mightiness can go by unnoticed and unspoken and unassumed. The fact it doesn't always roar doesn't detract from its sheer power. Consider the power of love; we don't ever doubt it exists but we know it does. Love is often an unnoticed, unspoken and unassumed power too. Electricity – we can't see the actual electrical current but it lights up whole towns and cities; it's powerful.

43

The power in you is always there, bubbling away. Even when you feel powerless, empty and depleted. It's there when you're taking some downtime, chilling, recharging and recovering. It's there, always.

You will have a gazillion examples of things you got through when you didn't think you could. Of obstacles that seemed unscalable, but you overcame them. Of things that felt impossible until they were done. Of ways you doubted yourself but showed up anyway. List 'em, reflect on them and use that list as a tool in your arsenal against those disempowering incessant nasty thoughts. You're so much more than those thoughts give you credit for. You're a mighty so-and-so, that's what you are.

Mightiness doesn't always roar.

You are not a burden

We're a polite bunch, aren't we?

We don't like to put people out. We like to help, to be useful and to be productive. We'll Google, we'll problem-solve, we'll read books. We try not to take up space or time. We put off the appointments. We'll apologise left, right and centre, for ev-ery-thing. We're apologetically us.

Which typically means that we carry burdens to prevent us from feeling like a burden.

And, boy, those burdens we carry? They don't half build up and weigh heavy. They're tiring and tiresome. And we all have them – those things that wear us down and wear us out. Those things that drain our emotions and cause us stress. Those things we could really do with some help/advice/guid-ance or closure on.

Here's the thing, though, that politeness and fear of being a burden generally bites us in the butt. We end up tripping ourselves up.

We don't consider that *not* being asked for help can cause worry or a sense of helplessness. We don't consider that mak-ing the appointment or taking up time can lessen the load before it gets any heavier. We're not setting others 'free' when we don't enlist their help – the burdens we bear are just growing into hard-to-keep-avoiding 'elephants in the room'. People like to help, just as we like to help others.

Because at some point we're probably going to need help with these burdens of ours. Just as others will need help with those burdens of theirs. And consider just for a moment what will you asking for help do?

It'll not only stop you bearing those burdens alone, but it'll prevent the damage they'll cause to you if you have to keep on carrying on, and the best bit is you'll be an example for someone else, who could also do with a little help. Courage is contagious, after all.

The next time someone asks if you're OK, bite back the automatic 'I'm fine' and give them a glimmer of a chance to be there for you – as you will no doubt be there for them one day too.

You are absolutely not a burden; you're carrying burdens. That's a mighty reframe if ever there was one.

People like to help, just as **we like to help** others.

Power up

Many of us can relate to the 'pendulum of self-care'.

We're feeling great, firing on all cylinders and self-care doesn't feel half as important. And then it swings right back to the opposite end of the scale and it becomes everything. It becomes the tool that helps us to hang on by our fingertips, the mode by which we gently ease our way back to health. It becomes a vital, life-saving act of self-kindness.

We pick it up and put it down depending on how great we feel, often experiencing a 'feast or famine' on our internal resources – the pendulum effect.

What if, rather than using self-care as a rescue remedy, we think of self-care as our daily power-ups – the actions we take to keep our power topped up?

For those of us well versed in *Super Mario*, it's akin to collecting hearts, coins, mushrooms, fire flowers and frog suits, *just in case* we might need them later. It's fun to collect them, there's a sense of achievement and you really just *never* know when you might find yourself in a sticky spot and really need a spangled fire flower to see off an enemy.

And, in a way, life imitates these games . . .

We can be certain that there will be something in our future that will test us and use up our feeling-well-ness. We all need allies to help us fight the enemies (depression, anxiety, boundaries and other things that deplete us). We can power up our strength by taking care of our emotional, mental, physical and social needs. We can think of hurdles as overcomable – with the right resources.

Surely, then, it makes complete sense that we power up at each and every opportunity, just like Mario would? So that when the bad times roll around (because they always do) we're as ready as we can be – we have magic powers stored up to dip into and power us through.

And doesn't 'power up' sound much more fun and less obligatory? It takes that sense of playfulness from gaming, of possibility, of hope, of there being infinite endings and applies it to real life.

We can change our view of self-care from being something we only do when we need to, to something that's fun to build up and collect as we go along. Like a real-life hero, which is what you are.

Your challenge, should you wish to accept it, is to start collecting those power-ups. What recharges, energises and powers you up?

4

Words for the days when you're experiencing negative thoughts

This chapter is full of guidance, insights
and takeaways to help you address and
reframe those negative thoughts as
and when they arise.

'Thinking positive' isn't always easy

The negative stuff tends to shine like a beacon, roar like a lion and refuse to retreat.

Positive stuff does happen, and we actively look for it, but it always feels outnumbered by the rough stuff, which starts to make us feel that we're doing something wrong, that we're broken, that we're really unlucky. Or all of the above.

What's so interesting is that the negative stuff seems to shape us too. We can all pinpoint a comment, a look, a something that made us adjust our sails ever so slightly. Whether it was ten minutes ago, ten weeks ago or ten years ago. There'll be something that we remember quite clearly, which affects how we go about our days or makes us second-guess ourselves.

There's a reason the negative weighs so heavy. And it's nothing to do with us as people; it's a biology thing.

Our brain has a negative bias. It's an evolutionary tool to keep us safe from danger, from waaay back in the cave and sabre-toothed tiger heyday. Our brain is wired to overplay the risks and remind us of the negative.

The trouble is, life has moved on, but that negative bias thing? It hasn't evolved, and it isn't half tiresome.

Life as we know it is loud and busy and full to the brim of information, different situations and people. And we're always, even if we don't realise it, interpreting ev-er-y darn thing to suss out the danger and to analyse the negative.

When you're told to 'think positive' and it feels a gazillion times harder than it sounds, know this: it *is* a gazillion times harder than it sounds.

It's not you, as a person. It's not you, in who you are. It's not that you're lacking in some magical and mystical 'think positive' skill set. It's your frickin' brain – it's doing what it's supposed to be doing, however truly exhausting that is.

Don't stop seeking the positive or challenging the negative thoughts and don't stop reaching out for help when they become the thing putting you in danger. But do try to stop thinking that you're at fault and do try to stop beating yourself up for seeing things in a greyer way than you think you should.

Try not to get it twisted

We have riotous imaginations that have created such things of wonder and beauty that the awe they inspire transcends time, countries and cultures.

The Egyptian pyramids
The Taj Mahal
The Colosseum
The Eiffel Tower
Brooklyn Bridge
La Sagrada Família
Countless books, songs, poetry, films, works of art

It's a never-ending list and there'll be things you'd add too.

On the flipside, we also have an ability to create grand internal stories of worry and fear with several interchanging scenarios. We'll invent scripts for what we will say and do should [this (probably never going to happen) undesired event] ever present itself. This imagination of ours, used in this way, can cause sleepless nights, anxiety and a state of mind that's disempowering and isolating, and makes us feel lacking, ashamed and less than.

Let's not get things twisted when your imagination takes a critical spin. Instead, reframe your thoughts more fairly:

- *A bad patch in a relationship doesn't mean it's doomed. Everything is sort-out-able if both parties are willing.*
- *Making a bad decision or three doesn't mean you're not competent. It means you didn't have the information you needed or perhaps you felt pressured to rush making it.*
- *Snapping at someone doesn't mean you're a nasty piece of work. It means you're depleted and need space.*
- *If life is weighing you down, it doesn't mean you're hopeless. It means you need some support.*

What are you bathing in?

There's a tidal motion to what we experience. Sometimes things are pretty darn terrific. Other times they're unsettling, uncertain and tricky. And there are times that bob along somewhere in the middle.

When the tide's out on the good times and the less desirable ones roll around, it's completely natural for us to feel worn out as we swim against the current, trying with all our might to reach calmer waters. It's understandable that waves of not-so-nice-to-feel emotions threaten to drown out the more welcome ones. It makes sense that every part of our being would resonate highly with someone else in the same situation.

If we were literally all at sea rather than these metaphorical examples, we'd be wanting and wishing with all our might for a life raft, a buoy. We'd want a break to catch our breath. And we'd want to get out of there pretty sharpish.

In times of instability our minds can be as tempestuous as the stormiest of seas. The thoughts can be menacing, savage, murky and wild. But there's a difference between experiencing a barrage of negative thoughts and bathing in them.

We could choose to bathe in them and let them cloud all

that we can see, touch and feel, or we could choose to be the sun. To create warmth, light and beauty for ourselves. Even from within the darkness.

It's difficult to turn the tide on the waves of negativity as they wash over us, and it's never quite as easy as 'thinking positive'. It's more a case of changing the channel – just as we can on the TV, our phones and the radio.

In the midst of the mind-mist we can choose positive action. We can choose to make, to bake, to connect, to write, to love, to plant, to shower ourselves gently in the things that bring comfort and warmth.

However ferocious the sea, you can and will find your way to calmer shores.

When it's blowing a gale outdoors, the clouds are dense and there's a downpour of rain, the sun doesn't cease to exist – we just can't see it. **We don't ever doubt it's there, though.**

Rebel

Everywhere we look – from carefully crafted Instagram feeds to hold-it-all-in underwear adverts to fear-mongering media headlines – there are brash messages telling us that we couldn't possibly be enough as we are. Here's *just* the lotion or potion or app to help with that. And it's all a load of codswallop, it really is.

It leads to us feeling judged and judgemental. We can't do right for doing wrong. It leaves that lingering feeling of wanting to hide because our reality is light years away from the reality we're presented with.

The worst thing about it is that the brash language and messaging completely outstay their welcome. They stick with us, permeating our thoughts and our choices. There's little wonder why we feel so wrong-footed, so unsure of ourselves and so scared of making mistakes; we see people being dragged through the mud for stepping out of line, of being *too* sure of themselves and for making even the littlest of mistakes.

It's partly why self-care feels awkward at times. And it's definitely why our initial reaction might be to scoff at loving ourselves. Those acts of self-kindness are so far removed and seem so far-fetched from what we're fed; the same media that writes an article about the gloriousness of self-care lambasts those in the media's eye for looking a tad dishevelled and uses a computer program to chop off bits of their body for the glossy photos. It's rife with mixed messaging, and we feel it when we see it, and we feel it when we try to be kinder to ourselves.

It's true, too, that there's something quite rebellious about being kind to ourselves – it goes against everything we see in shops, supermarkets, online and in print. Rebellion versus conformity. Shrugging off those weighty shoulds and instead going where our heart guides us. Not wanting to be just like [insert whoever here] because we're stepping into and owning who we are. Mavericking it to a time where there's enough self-love around that it spills over into every interaction, every pathway, every choice, every place and every person we meet.

Rebel against the societal 'norms' by:

Choosing self-forgiveness over self-punishment.
Choosing self-compassion over self-frustration.
Choosing self-kindness over listening to the inner trolls.
Choosing to give your high-five moments more headspace than the wobbles.
Choosing where you give away your yeses.
Choosing to give yourself the benefit of the doubt.
Choosing you more.

*Choosing to see the potential in yourself rather than where
you might be stuck.*

*Choosing to trust yourself over those weird mixed
messages.*

*Choosing to accept that you are so, so, so, so, so enough
as you are.*

We might not always be able to change the world around us,
but we can absolutely change the world within us (which,
y'know, ends up changing the world around us anyway!).

Definitely don't feed the ants

Now then, nobody likes an infestation. Whether that's an infestation of cockroaches or ants or negative thoughts. It's not really where we'd like to be, in the middle of any of that.

Trouble is, our brain has other ideas. It's not evolved quite as fast as everything else and it likes to constantly and consistently point out things that could be negative or dangerous, to try to keep us safe. In some ways it's very kind of it to worry so. But we're generally not still living in caves and having to deal with those prehistoric day-to-day battles for survival. It's not got the memo that times have changed.

The trouble with these thoughts is that they're automatic: Automatic Negative Thoughts (ANTs). No matter who we are, no matter our circumstances, our titles, our positions, our lifestyles, we all have them.

For some of us, though, those ANTs are an infestation and it's pretty darned painful and noisy.

In the midst of such uncertainty here are some ways we might be able to halt or draw up the drawbridge, to quell the invasion of negative thoughts:

1. *Our thoughts lie to us. Often. Try writing them down and ask yourself if they're really true. Like, honestly, really, really? Chances are they're not. Your brain is just wanting you to sit up, take stock and evaluate. Sometimes the act of writing thoughts down and evaluating them is enough to quieten them.*

2. *Disrupt thoughts in their tracks. We can all remember a time when we were feeling pretty grotty and then something happened that was exciting and helped us to feel better. That was our thoughts being disrupted, and we can actually do it for ourselves if we're self-aware enough to realise that the ANTs are approaching. Different strokes for different folks here, but you could try a replacement. When the 'I am so [insert something really mean here]' thoughts pop up, consider repeating a nicer one, such as 'I am strong/kind/funny/fun etc.'.*

3. *Collate evidence against them: a folder on your computer, a camera reel of kind messages, a corkboard full of letters, positive words and feedback. Look at it when the ANTs start to swarm.*

4. *Stand up for yourself and argue back. Take the thought and raise it. So, if the recurring thought is that you messed up, and the feeling you get is that it just goes to show how useless you are, stop, take a breath and argue back. 'I might have messed up, but I really did try my best and do my best. I know differently now so I'll do*

differently if and when there's a next time.'

5. *Be careful of what's around you. If the people you spend time with are always putting you down, if you have a crappy boss, if you engage in any diatribe on social media, if you love nothing more than to get involved in gossip and judge and put others down, if what you read and watch is full of betrayal, gore and sadness, then you're likely to be feeding the ANTs. Flip the switch and surround yourself with what'll lift you, not limit you.*

ANT infestations are disempowering; they leave us feeling exhausted and at war with ourselves. When our external worlds are hostile, they play into our thoughts and feelings. If we can prevent any invasion on our thoughts, even just a little, we can gift ourselves a little more peace of mind.

Get curious

Reflecting back over our lives doesn't always end very well. We might get drawn into the decisions and actions that changed our trajectories in ways we're discontent with. Ruminating often taps into that self-critical inner voice that crushes us down with all the things we wish we'd done differently.

If we're going through a stage where life feels proper rubbish, then there will be some rational answers in the looking back, but only if we do so with an investigative hat on, not that nasty ruminating one that just seems to diminish any sense of self-belief, self-love and self-esteem we were holding on to.

When we become curious, interested in patterns, as inspectors and investigators in our own lives, we're able to realise that our life doesn't need a complete overhaul, because the smallest of tweaks can lead to the biggest of changes.

An inspecting and investigative eye creates an awareness, fosters responsibility over our choices and actions, and helps us to analyse and rationalise in a way that our emotion-led selves aren't always able to.

To help engage our innate curiosity, it helps to track stuff, to journal our moods, our habits, the people we've been around, the things we've been up to, because that is valuable data when it comes to finding patterns. Perhaps every time we spend time with Great-aunt Edna, whose belittling comments and critical voice drags us down, we see a plunge in our mood. If we'd captured that data, we'd notice that pattern and could either stop seeing her altogether or at the very least decrease how often.

Perhaps we're in our element when we're up to our knees in paint and that's when we feel the most fulfilled and at peace. Those journalled days would surely show a boost in our mood.

You don't even need a fancy notebook to do this; you can use the notes on your phone, free habit-tracker apps, printer paper or any way that suits you. But give it a go, just for a week: jot down how you've been feeling, ponder over the whys for that day, track your habits, write about who you were with, what you were doing and how it all felt, and then leave it.

At the end of the seven days, read back over your notes with your detective inspector hat on and see what pops out for you. Are there are some habits you'd like to change? Some relationships that don't really bring out the best in you? What are the obstacles, the high-five moments and the circumstances surrounding those? What's going well, and what's not, and commit to making even the teeniest change for yourself possible.

Remember, though: detective inspector you is a compassionate, kind and curious soul who is able to cast a critical, questioning and interested eye over the data, but who doesn't cast aspersions, judgements or self-criticism (just in case your inner troll tries to dive in and sabotage what could be a really useful exercise).

The weeds and the seeds

It's gotta be said that there's nothing wrong with weeds – in theory. There are some proper pretty ones around, but what defines a weed is that it's something that grows where you don't want it to grow. And, boy, when they grow do they *grow*. It takes patience, time, elbow grease and repeated effort to remove them because if you don't do it regularly, they'll outgrow and kill anything that you've intentionally planted.

Our negative thoughts and self-chatter are exactly the same. We know when this has happened too – that flash of inspiration, an idea that pops into our heads, a daydream or a bolt of excitement that all too often is followed by the self-doubt, worry, crisis of confidence and eleventy squillion reasons not to do the very thing that moments ago we felt and thought was amazing.

The ideas, the lofty goals, allowing ourselves to daydream and scheme, and the things that excite us – they're the seeds. The stuff that follows that bursts our balloon – they're the weeds.

When we consider this from a rational viewpoint it seems obvious that we'd want more of the seeds, please. But has it occurred to you that sometimes we choose the weeds? It's sadly true. The weeds, when kept unchecked, unfiltered and un-dealt with, outgrow and kill any seeds that we've intentionally planted (and unintentionally, because sometimes amazing things pop into our heads in the shower, for instance).

We've all got a back catalogue of dreams we shelved because those damn weeds told us we couldn't, that it wouldn't work, that we're not enough, that we'd fail and so on and so on, and we believed them. They grew so ferociously that they knocked the oxygen and life outta the good stuff.

There are theories aplenty that talk about how our dreams, daydreams, gut, instincts and desires are our purpose and path – that's where we could head to, if only we could tame those blinkin' weeds, eh?!

Well, the good news is that we abso-flippin'-lutely can dilute and lessen them. The harder news is that it takes patience, time, elbow grease and conscious and repeated effort.

We can do this by taking care of the information that comes in; is it all doomy and gloomy and playing into any internal fears you have or is it inspiring, uplifting and teaching you a good thing or two?

- *What about the people you hang out with?*
- *Are they the sort to pooh-pooh your dreams or are they a right ol' encouraging, go-get-'em-tiger sort?*
- *How do you handle compliments? Do you ping-pong*

'em right back or do you graciously accept the gift of kind words?

- *And what about that negative self-chatter? Are you collecting mental or physical evidence to support it or curating a box/folder/pinboard full of evidence of the times you kicked ass, achieved, overcame, did the thing you thought you could not do?*
- *What's your knee-jerk self-chatter? Is it to let the weeds rambunctiously gather momentum or do you try to be mindful and peacefully let those thoughts go, losing steam as they drift away?*

Pay attention to the seeds, and create an internal environment where they can bloom and flourish. And as for the weeds, you know what to do with those.

It takes **patience, time,** elbow grease and **conscious** and repeated **effort to fight negative** thoughts and chatter.

You are worthy of compassion too

We push, pull, strive and we keep on keeping on.

When it comes to compassion, we're scrumdiddlyumptious at handing it out willy-nilly. It comes from an empathy of how rotten things can get and that understanding, lived experience and pain memory means that we'll do our best to alleviate the suffering of others whenever we get the chance.

And that's so bloomin' lovely – it highlights the best of humanity and the magical transformational powers of kindness.

We also see how it can affect a child's development when they're starved of kindness and connection and compassion. It impacts how their emotions are processed, their understanding of boundaries, how safe a child might feel, their sense of self, relationships, confidence and behaviour.

It makes sense then that when we withhold kindness and compassion from ourselves it might impact a great many aspects of our lives and how we feel about ourselves.

The inner critic, the inner troll, the inner perfectionist – those things are primarily a primal way of our brains keeping us safe, but they don't serve us. They don't nurture us. Tough love seldom does.

There's an influx of 'what other people are up to' in our lives and it's proper difficult to turn a blind eye to it. We're well aware of the leaps and bounds, achievements and butt-kicking shenanigans our peers are making. All the while we feel as though we're tiptoeing forward with trepidation and a palpable fear of making a mistake, of not matching up, of not being enough. That doesn't half weigh heavy.

Of all the people who truly deserve your compassion it's you. *It's always been you.*

The benefit of the doubt
The reassuring words
The forgiveness and acceptance

You deserve it, and, even better, it's all yours for the taking.

When you catch your inner troll being a ferocious troll-like beast, slay it. Kill it with kindness and then apply that kindness to every dilly-dally, stumble and fall. Let's end this self-compassion drought and flood our lives with the kindness we totally deserve. Here are some small actions you can take to tackle your inner troll:

- *Write the words 'I am worthy/enough/clever/strong' on your mirror so you see it every day.*

- *Change your phone wallpaper to one with an empowering phrase (take a photo of one of the quote pages in this book!).*
- *Celebrate every tiny victory for an hour, afternoon or day.*

5

Words for the days when you've made a mistake or two

When you're laden with guilt, embarrassment or shame, dive deep into the soothing words within this chapter for a reprieve and the chance to see things differently.

Don't let the past trip you up

One of the things that can stunt our growth, halt our progress and weaken our ability to shine as brightly as we have the potential to do, is the past.

The very nature of life is its endless inability to stay still. Even when we're still, things evolve, meander and flex around us. When we feel still, our brain and body continue working to keep us ticking over, renewing and recharging. There is no true stillness – it might be microscopic and unintelligible at times, but we're always changing.

We flow the way we're directed and when we look back, particularly at missed chances and romances, the guilt and the silt, the regrets and the upsets, then we risk losing sight of where we are right now and of where we'd like to be.

The past builds us, moulds us and influences us, but it doesn't define us. Who we were yesterday is not who we are today. Who we are today is not who we'll be tomorrow.

The past *can* trip us up. It can weigh heavy and it can weigh us down. But we can only change what's ahead of us. We still get to write *those* chapters.

And there is absolutely no shame in asking for help with

that; after all, sometimes there are things that have caused considerable trauma, pain and hurt, that we just don't know how to navigate. Asking for directions when we're lost saves us from wasting more time, energy and pain.

You might feel it but you're never, ever broken – resetting, unpeeling the layers, unfolding, learning, taking a break, taking stock, calling in the cavalry, mending, but not broken.

When life gives you lemons, know this: you'll never be given a lemon bigger than you; there's nothing you can't overcome – honestly. Believe in yourself, believe that you're the best lemon lobber in the land, ask for help when the lemons get too much, and do your best. It's all anyone can ever ask of you (yourself included).

We can only change what's ahead of us. We still get to write *those* chapters.

The stumbles and the crumbles

The stumbles in life are an inevitable part of it. It's natural to experience uncertainty, to make mistakes and for things to not work out as planned. The only thing we can do to avoid them is to not do anything new or different, to avoid growth and challenges. But then we get stuck, cast our dreams aside and ignore the changes we need to make, so, yup, stumbles are to be expected.

The crumbles, however, not so much. The crumbles can be painful, embarrassing and can cause emotional hangovers. They can cripple relationships and they can cause us to feel guilty and ashamed. We've all crumbled and experienced the walls crashing in as life topples us over. These crumbles tend to be caused by excess: excess weight on our shoulders (problems, responsibility, expectations); excess bottling up of emotion inside; excess negativity (external or internal); excess stumbles; excess sensory stuff; excess people-ing; excess insomnia – the list goes on.

The crumbles can be avoided, but in order to avoid them we've got to get real with who we are and what we need. Oftentimes it's the crumbling that highlights that something has gone awry. It's only when we analyse the precursor to it that we can pinpoint what caused it.

What went on before the crumble? Had stress increased? Perhaps you had taken on too much? Maybe your needs hadn't been met? Take some time to consider what it was that toppled you. And why.

That information is golden because it paves the way for supportive action: asking for help, building in time for quietude, buying tools to help protect our senses (noise-cancelling earphones, etc.) – self-care systems that help support all your quirks and needs and protect you from that crumbling.

Ride the crumbles as best you can, seeking comfort and reassurance to help you through. Blast yourself with kindness when they happen and when you've ridden the storm, *as you absolutely definitely will.*

Endless guilt trips are not the answer

Guilt is an odd emotion that can stun us into staying right where we are. But it can also instigate change.

There are so many reasons and ways that we might feel guilty:

Guilt about compromises or sacrifices we might have had to make.
Guilt about the mistakes we've made.
Guilt about when we've been too [insert adjective here].
Guilt about what we said or didn't say.
Guilt about what we thought or didn't think.
Guilt for not doing or being enough.
Guilt for what we have or don't have.

Guilt magnifies shame.

Then there's that self-guilt when we take on responsibility for other people's actions. We may feel guilt when someone barges into us, when someone says something hurtful to us or when we feel we're taking up too much space.

We can't half tie ourselves up in knots with this guilt stuff.

So much so that it debilitates and humiliates.

Guilt keeps us down; it drowns us in its waves, and from that place no meaningful change can ever occur. We can mentally beat ourselves up for things over and over, and it doesn't change anything that's gone before, but, by golly it changes what's coming for us, and not in a good way.

You see, if we let it, guilt will knock us to our knees and keep us there. It will overpower and disempower until we run out of power.

Choosing to bathe in guilt is like trying to clean a window with a mouldy old cloth and a bucket of muddy water. We're not going to end up with the outcome that we're after.

Try to change the gear from reverse (because that's what guilt often does to us – it keeps us in the past, playing a video in our brain on repeat of all the coulda, shoulda, wouldas) into first gear. First gear is when we step back and look at the source of guilt with a compassionate 'How am I going to learn from this?' stance. A stance that will empower, educate and encourage. We can use our hindsight to change our future in the way we'd like.

Guilt is an odd emotion that can stun us into staying right where we are. But it can also instigate change.

Tough love is rarely the answer

It's not something that we crave is it, tough love? The discerning cold approach. Being pushed towards a desired outcome in a harsh, fractious and unassisted way. Stripped of ballyhoo and cheer, even if there's undoubtedly underlying goodwill and love at the core. It conjures up imagery of someone scared of putting a step wrong, of a motivation born from a desire to please or to avoid reproach.

When we see someone walking, we're seeing the culmination of hundreds of wobbly footsteps and not-quite-there-yet footsteps that they made, or didn't quite make, as a toddler.

When we hear someone talking, we're hearing the outcome of all those practised 'ma-ma's and 'ga-ga's and 'woof-woof's and the stringing together of syllables until they eventually become coherent sentences.

When we read a letter, we're reading the results of hours spent learning how to craft the ABCs, of getting to grips with the nuances of our language and of having mistakes crossed out in red ink by a teacher.

When we see people achieving and doing and being, and then feel overwhelmed by the chasm of where we are and where they are, we're comparing what we don't yet know with what they've learned.

We don't know what we don't know.

And learning? It takes time. It involves a willingness to be not great at something. It requires us to embrace the vulnerability that can come with starting something. It asks us to forgive ourselves the stumbles and the crumbles as we navigate uncharted territory. It means we have to get comfy with the unknown until it becomes known.

When we cast ourselves in an unfavourable light because of what we don't know, we're being really unfair to ourselves. We're also downplaying the toil, sweat, grunt work, tears, courses, classes, book reading and YouTubing that took a person from A to B. We're forgetting that when toddlers stumble over their feet and mumble over their tongue, their *trying* is celebrated. The trying is actively encouraged. There's applause waaaay before the 'thing' is learned.

Tough love is very rarely going to nurture us in quite the encouraging and motivating way a bucketload of empathy, kindness and patience can. When you're at the starting line of something completely new, remember that you can do masses of things now that you once could not. All you had to do was try and try and try and try some more again. Keep a log of all the ways you've been trying, growing and improving lately, including the effort to try in the first place.

Allow yourself the space to wobble, make mistakes, waver and to not know whatever it is you want to know without these tough-love shenanigans.

Would you say it to a friend?

Would you berate a friend who was stuck? Call them stupid, thick, pathetic, lazy?

Would you push a friend to achieve more, more, more when you could see that what they really needed was to rest up?

Would you make negative comments about their appearance?

Would you bring up that mistake they made back in a day long gone and keep relentlessly reminding them of it over and over and over and over?

Would you smash their dreams to smithereens by telling them they're not good enough nor worthy?

No, no, no, no and no.

You simply wouldn't. You wouldn't because it would be unkind – downright cruel, in fact. You just wouldn't kick someone who was down, and a friendship wouldn't bloom within that toxicity.

Yet these are just a few examples of the internal struggles and internal dialogues we dish out to ourselves daily. We continue to kick ourselves when we're down, over and over again. *We* can't grow within that toxicity.

We deserve the same compassion, kindness, patience, empathy and encouragement that we cast outwards so freely. So your new rule of thumb from here on in is: if you wouldn't say it to a friend, don't say it to yourself. Be your own BFF in your thoughts, actions and choices. We deserve to bloom.

And, no, it won't be easy, because creating new habits never is. But it will be worth the effort, because kindness is like sprinkling fairy dust over things – it's magic.

You're doing your best

It's a weird thing that we do, this holding ourselves to exemplary, dizzily high standards. No matter what we're going through and dealing with, we hold these self-standards and self-expectations steadfast and then use them as a tool with which to crucify ourselves.

Let's be frank for a moment: this is the epitome of unkindness and shows a severe lack of compassion, empathy and patience. You'd never, ever treat anyone else who was going through hardships in this way.

We can't be hunky-dory and firing on all cylinders all the time. *Nobody can.*

There will be seasons of our lives just as there are seasons in nature. Some will feel stark, unforgiving and stormy. Others will seem plain sailing, warm and abundant.

We're going to have to flex in every way to whichever season our lives are in. Sunny times? Yay – go and make hay while the sun shines. Not-so-sunny times? Stop thinking about being your best and *do your best*. Lower your standards of yourself when the environment around you isn't conducive to blooming – we don't expect other things in nature to bloom in the conditions they weren't made for.

The tricky thing about self-expectations is they rarely come backed up with a contingency plan. We seldom make allowances for ourselves when unforeseen stuff casts our plans adrift. We plough on and on and on, not stopping to recalibrate, to take stock. We don't see that it's not our lack of anything that's changed the expected outcomes; it's all those variables we couldn't possibly have known about or factored in. When our environments change unexpectedly, we are allowed to unexpectedly change and renegotiate our goals, deadlines, plans and dreams. Not stop or drop them, just give ourselves some leeway.

Please don't be so hard on yourself.

Lower your standards
of yourself when the
environment around
you isn't conducive
to blooming.

Shower yourself in self-kindness

There's a lot of talk at the moment about self-love. Where we totally and utterly accept and love ourselves for who we are in the here and now. And it's a wonderful concept.

But when we're in the pits of a dark and murky time we don't tend to feel all that great about ourselves. Self-love feels like such a gargantuan leap from where we are. We might even be finding self-like to be a bit of a stretch.

How on earth do we get from where we are to a place of self-love? Self-like even?

We shower in self-kindness every single day. Even when we feel unworthy of it, especially when we feel unworthy of it. We practise, practise and we practise some more.

This is when our actions of self-kindness can speak louder than the words we tell ourselves.

It's about creating a new norm, a new reality, a new set of habits that support who we are. It'll feel awkward, as though we're going against the grain. It's something we're not taught, so it can feel clumsy and inauthentic. But, by golly it works.

Self-kindness looks like:

Taking what we need
Honouring how we feel
Setting and asserting boundaries
Saying goodbye to toxic environments
Being mindful of our self-talk
Meaningful connection
Disconnection
Hydration
Asking for help
Accepting help
Soothing and comforting anchors spread throughout
   your day
Taking breaks
Replacing those holey slippers
Treating yourself to something
Making time for fun
Being honest
Celebrating our achievements, no matter how small

So many of us are taught to be kind to others and we nail it, but when it comes to being kind to ourselves we get stuck. It's never too late to learn or unlearn this stuff. Start today. Start small. Set up a mini self-kindness system with non-negotiable reminders in your phone, your diary, in Trello or Asana. It might be an alien habit in a world that actively encourages us to be mean to ourselves and to dislike ourselves, but it's a much-needed habit of protection, compassion and reflection.

You unequivocally *do* deserve self-kindness, especially when your knee-jerk reaction is to say that you don't.

You do, you do, you do, you do, you do, you do, you do, you do. We all do.

6

Words for the days when you feel you've lost your way

If you're feeling as though you could really do with a compass and map to help you navigate this thing called life, then this chapter is exactly what you're looking for.

The lies we tell ourselves

There's nothing like telling lies or being lied to, to wreak havoc in our relationships. Lies damage integrity, trust, credibility and the value and power of our words to come and words gone by.

But perhaps worst of all are the lies we tell ourselves. The living so out of sync with who we are. The conceding of ourselves as we compromise who we are again and again and again. The going with the flow of everything else, when really, if we were following our inner compass, we'd be going against the grain. The erosion of our sense of self and all that comes with that: the lowering of self-esteem, self-worth, self-confidence. The feeling of inauthenticity and doing our utmost to measure up to the standards set by others.

It's a load of codswallop really, this lying to ourselves malarkey, and it's as damaging to the relationship we have with ourselves and our sense of self as it is when we tell lies or are lied to. We damage our own integrity, credibility and self-trust, and undermine the promises we make to ourselves. We start to doubt our very own dedication and motivation, feeling like a failure before we've got going.

The lies we tell ourselves aren't always black and white; they can be ambiguous and more about what we do than what we say. Such as hiding our bushel to make others feel more comfortable, self-deprecation so that we don't appear too big for our boots, saying yes when we mean no, saying no when we mean yes, telling ourselves that we'll do differently next time and not, looking to others for the answers we already hold inside, de-prioritising our priorities to prioritise other people's, plastering on a smile to mask the frown lines or tear tracks, not paying attention to the cues or instincts or heart feelings.

And it's the heart feelings that matter so, so much. The following of your heart rather than your head. Coming from a place of complete and utter honesty in all that you are and all that you aren't.

Step into that stuff. Embrace who you are and who you aren't without judgement, deceit and criticism. Be true to you.

Your inner GPS system

That feeling that we've taken a wrong turn, made a mistake and aren't at all sure what we're doing.

Perhaps we're feeling detached, disorientated and completely unsure what to do next. Maybe we are looking outside ourselves for all the answers, caught up in comparisonitis and feeling somewhat lacking.

It feels proper uncomfortable to feel any of those things, but it is also quite normal. People just don't like showing this side of their lives. In a world where there's a barrage of opinions, cultures, societal shoulds, and no road map handed to us at birth, it's normal that we will lose our way at times. Many times over.

We're built with an inner GPS system of sorts. It's a homing beacon that helps guide us to make the choices which are right for us. Our body and mind communicate with us when we're hungry or when we're thirsty, but they also communicate other things that serve us too (although they don't always feel so helpful at the time). Anger, resentment, frustration, loneliness and overwhelm are just some of the cues we receive that things have gone a bit wonky-tonk.

As babies our inner GPS is firing on all cylinders; we express what we need without a filter, loudly. Then, slowly over time, our GPS signal loses its strength because we learn to stop listening to it and we're taught to fall in line. It starts with how we're nurtured and 'shown' the way – school plays a big part in that we're surrounded by peers and teachers who need us to focus on learning what the curriculum states we ought to be learning. The peer pressure we feel as a student never goes away because we're social beings and, lo and behold, by the time we're grown-ups we've learned to stop trusting ourselves and spend our adult years trying to unpick and to tune back in.

Is it any wonder, then, that we often feel unanchored and lost?

Yet being lost is a great big mammoth-sized opportunity to recalibrate.

Try not to get lost in the feeling of being lost. Losing our way is part and parcel of finding our way. Life is very much trial and error, and the growing pains teach us what isn't right for us – not because we're not worthy, not because we're not enough, but because *those choices aren't good enough for us*. Take time to rest and then set about tuning in to what *you* need and what the right turn is for *you*.

One of the best ways to do this is by making a list of three things you'd like to achieve in the next hour, day or week, and then for each come up with one step you can make towards that goal. These steps can be really small; it can just be getting up from the sofa! But schedule it into your diary or calendar and know that you're beginning to find your way.

You're allowed to change your mind a **gazillion** times until you find the right way for you.

Turn up your volume

Feeling heard, understood and listened to is all kinds of wonderful.

But do you know what's more powerful? Hearing, understanding and listening to ourselves. And we so often don't do it.

Consider the times you may have been persuaded against your better judgement to do something that turned out all hooky. The times someone asked you to do something and you felt your stomach drop but did it anyway. The times you bit your lip so as not to cause conflict but then experienced that inner torment as you replayed the situation over and over and over again. All the times your gut instincts and intuition said one thing and you did the opposite.

You absolutely know what's best for you if you tune in and then turn up your volume.

There will be opportunities, decisions, choices and outcomes that make you feel buoyed up, energised, excited and alight with what could be. Similarly there will be opportunities, decisions, choices and outcomes that make you feel trapped, in a corner, contracted, your mojo ablaze with shoulds and oughts.

Once you tune in to that inner voice of yours, you won't ever want to tune out, for it is wise, always has your back and cares about your happiness. And, nope, I'm not talking about that fearful voice that pipes up; I'm talking about those visceral reactions we so often ignore, the dreams and hopes that don't go away no matter how much we misalign with them, and those ideas you have in the shower that make you feel giddy – *that's* the voice I'm talking about. And you have one, we all have one, and now it's time to let that voice be heard.

Pay attention to how you react to what's asked of you or by you, to the pangs of envy and to the whispers of your heart. Lean hard into the buoyant and the joyous. Hear and feel the things that you love, and turn up the volume of those things as loudly as you dare.

Permission isn't needed

People aren't backward in coming forward with their opinions, their shoulds and their perspectives on how our stories ought to unfold.

Sometimes these are masked as judgement-laden curiosity: 'You're approaching your second wedding anniversary, will there soon be a baby on the way?'

As surprise: 'You're going to drop out of uni and do what?!'

Or the ol' 'If it were me, I'd . . .'

Unsolicited advice or judgement with icing, sprinkles and cherries on top.

More often than not these come from well-meaning relatives who express their agreement or disagreement with our life choices. But they can come from anywhere: friends, magazines, social media, societal cultures, every which way.

And it can be a heavy burden to bear that we might not be meeting expectations of us. That we might not match up with the 'master life plan' (as though everyone got given a handbook about life that we're not privy to). That we're a disappointment. In fact, there are times when we fear that disappointment so tangibly that we hide who we are. We compromise our truth because we're fearful of the backlash.

And to be quite frank it's a repeated travesty that we all know too well. It smarts, it adds friction, we feel 'fake', we feel lost, we feel resentful, and it keeps us in 'line' – whatever this 'line' is. It keeps us unhappy too.

Those remarks, looks, comments and judgements often come from a place of regret, control or assumptions that aren't for us to heal, mend or adhere to.

We don't half deserve more. Much more. We deserve to go the whole hog and live our lives as truthfully, authentically and freely as is humanly possible.

The only permission we need to do that is ours. We can go our own way.

We're all leaders here

When we think of leaders we think of the heads of state, the big CEOs, the Greta Thunbergs, the inventors or the people who lead the masses – whether that's in a positive or quite baffling or scary way. What we don't consider is our own leadership roles in society. Most of the time we might not have ever considered ourselves as leaders.

'Me, a leader?' you ask. Yes, you. Absolutely and unequivocally you.

If you have any influence whatsoever over those around you, you're a leader. Whether you lead people up the garden path (I doubt very much you do that, but some people do) or lead them in a way that inspires, motivates, encourages and teaches them, you're a leader.

If your words have ever lit up someone's eyes with smiles, bolstered someone who is flailing, encouraged a child to try again, soothed and eased pain, provided hope, stoked the fire of their dreams, reached out and helped someone, acted with compassion in the face of adversity, held someone's hand in the darkness, then you are a leader.

Leadership isn't always a position we hold with fancy-schmancy titles; it's the energy, the commitment, how we communicate, our ability to bring calm or whip people into a frenzy. It's the influence we have over others and the responsibility, value and care we place on that influence on our peers, our children, our colleagues, our communities, our teams and our nations.

In the midst of a world that feels as though it's unravelling, consider the impact you might have on those around you.

Turn helplessness into helpfulness.
Choose your actions to speak louder than your words.
Have good intent in your clout.
Choose mutual communication over control.
Empathy always, over invalidation of feelings.
Pass what you've learned forward.
Offer your hindsight as another's foresight.
Give others who are more unfortunate a leg up.
Bolster, encourage, connect and choose your words
    carefully.

If your words have ever lit up someone's eyes with **smiles, bolstered** someone who is flailing, acted with **compassion** in the face of adversity, held someone's **hand in the darkness**, then you are a **leader**.

7

Words for the days when you feel stuck and frustrated

You must be feeling discontent, discouraged, irked and stumped right now to have found your way to this chapter. This chapter could well hold the clues to help you unlock the answer you're looking for.

Golden nuggets of hindsight

Our hindsight is as valuable to us as is it to others. It's rich with knowledge about what did and didn't work for us. And that's like gold dust.

There's a common reflex that happens when we find ourselves at our wits' end after one of life's hard knocks. The embers of self-distrust sneak in. An internal dialogue pipes up with all the things we could or should have done differently. Self-blame and self-chastising, and viewing our gut instincts, our intuition, our experiences and our ways of thinking with suspicion. We lose trust in the person we can trust above all others – ourselves.

After all, we got ourselves into this mess, right?! The mess feels awful, it feels inescapable, horrid. While we feel tangled, wrangled and mangled, we also need to remember that it's all definitely sort-out-able.

It's one thing to reflect and learn but quite another to poke and prod and lament our actions. Looking back can propel us forward or it can trip us up. Ruminating, beating ourselves up or layering on the regrets keeps us stuck. It uses up valuable energy, motivation and solutions-focused headspace.

Instead, we can take our hindsight and use it as a tool to help us become unstuck. We can look back and see that our past is full of golden nuggets of hindsight that speak so loudly as to what did and didn't work for us. Importantly, too, that same hindsight proves that we have been stuck and become unstuck many times before.

Change the story

Have you ever been listening to the radio and a tune comes on that you haven't heard for donkey's years? You start singing and you realise that despite the years that have passed you've still got the lyrics down pat.

Our memories are funny ol' things; we can remember the lyrics from a song from years gone by but not what we had for breakfast last week. We can remember that exact look and the exact words that hurt us aeons ago but not remember to send off that letter that's sat right beside the door (which we passed on our way out!).

Have you noticed, though, that it's the great and the fugly that we remember with ease? Not the mundane, the plethora of grey. And, even more annoyingly, is when we talk to our friends or family about a shared time and their memory of it is so darned different. That's perspective for ya – we apply different meanings and different emotions to things than other people might.

Our perspectives are made up of how we've lived up to now, the experiences and culture, and how we've been nurtured, that have shaped us. The best thing about perspective, though, is that at any given moment we can change it. We have this re-ally quite clever ability to see things from different viewpoints. To change the story.

That's all 'thinking outside the box' is; it's taking a different angle to find solutions and problems.

And we can all do that. We all get stuck from time to time; that's growth, that's life and that's natural. Sometimes it helps us to talk about it (a problem halved . . .), sometimes we ask for advice or read books or watch YouTube videos (gaining a differing perspective), and sometimes the answers come to us when we're in the shower or doing something completely unrelated to the stuck-ness.

If you're stuck right now and it's the same kind of stuck that's been stuck for a while, what can you do or who can you speak with that will help you see a different perspective? What can you try that you've not tried before (perhaps you've written off the very thing as 'not for you' without giving it a go)? How can you change the story you tell yourself?

You won't stay stuck for ever, though. Remember all of it – the good, the bad and the ugly – passes at some point.

We all get stuck
from time to time,
that's growth,
that's life
and that's **natural**.

It might take a reframe

When we have a lofty goal or dream, we're filled with motivation and passion to reverse-engineer it and break it down into the tiniest of chunks and to make progress, day by day, step by step. We might meander and need to realign, we might make mistakes and we might need help, but it's all in the name of that goal-getting fun, right? We don't ever expect to get from where we are to where the lofty goal is overnight. We appreciate there's work to be done, growth to grow through and learning curves to ride. We know that it's going to be a stretch.

Problems, on the other hand . . . well, they're not something we seek nor want in our lives. They're irritating, frustrating and distracting. They can come out of nowhere and demand all our attention and cojones. They're a downright nuisance. Oh, and they don't wait their turn. Oh no, they pour right in, soaking us in despair.

The thing is, there's little that separates a goal and a problem. They both require patience, elbow grease, inner grit, riding the learning curves, an overcoming of something.

How we address 'em, though, that's where the difference can lie. We address a goal with passion but a problem with shame. We choose the goal but the problem seems to find us. We're full of self-compassion with the goal-getting but full of self-criticism when we have a problem to solve. A goal feels empowering, but a problem disempowering. There's an epic mindset battle at play but the secret to grabbing that goal or pounding the problem is that the exact same mindset is required to work through both.

This means we might need to dilly our approach and dally our mindsets. You see, there's nothing at all that you can't handle. Nothing. Even if you're currently faced with the murkiest, overwhelmingly atrocious looming problems of all, you can and you will get through them.

Probably not as quickly as you'd like. Possibly not without help. And most definitely not without learning a thing or two. It might take a reframe or a problem rename, but you will get through it, slowly but surely. You will. You absolutely, most definitely will.

The secret to grabbing that **goal** or **pounding the problem** is that the exact same mindset is required to work through both.

Rose-tinted specs

The worst thing about low self-esteem and low self-worth is that it polarises our perspectives on who we are versus who other people are, but also on how other people see us versus how we see ourselves.

There is a discord, a sense of detachment, a feeling of confusion and a belief that we're lacking as people.

We cast a critical eye over everything we are and everything we do, yet pop on our rosiest rose-tinted spectacles as we place our loved ones on a pedestal. We're never going to match up unless we can find a way to view us, and them, with the same specs on.

Discomfort also comes a-running when we're with other people, because their words of encouragement, their words of comfort, their awe in the things we do, the way they might care for us and their belief in us is so mismatched with how we see ourselves – it's as if they're talking about a completely different person.

Those 'other' people are us. What they are to us, we are to them – loved ones. And the thought of them beating themselves up, being so critical, feeling so darned undeserving of the good stuff, makes us feel really sad. Yet we seem to find it hard to afford ourselves the same compassion and kindness.

When we come from a place of not feeling enough, it affects absolutely everything: our thoughts, our decisions, the things we do and say, our boundaries, how we treat ourselves, how we reflect and how we look ahead. We might feel stuck and limited by that too, as though we're never going to have what it takes to do XYZ, to be XYZ or to have XYZ.

Changing our viewpoint isn't ever going to be easy. Habits are notoriously difficult to break. Our brains, as magnificent as they can be, can work against us. The struggle convinces us that we were right to begin with: that we're not enough, worthy or deserving after all. And that's a pile of poo.

Everyone (yep, that includes you) is deserving of the good stuff: good health, happiness, laughter, being who we want to be and realising our dreams. Don't forget, if it's true for 'them', it's also true for us. It's one of those universal law things (and, by the way, we're not any less deserving because we've made mistakes along the way – we've ALL made those and they're lessons, not something that diminishes our worthiness).

When we feel stuck in a rut and the critical thoughts are loud and the self-doubt stifling, we need to try to turn the tables. We can do this by taking the advice we would give to others, by acknowledging the self-doubt but not giving it the pleasure of listening to it (it's almost always wrong), and when we can't muster the self-belief for ourselves we can borrow the belief in us from others.

When we've lost our rose-tinted, looking-inward spectacles, we can borrow those from someone else too.

Coulds not shoulds

There is so much in life that's out of our control: traffic jams, other people's behaviour and choices, the school curriculum, the health of others – so, so, so much.

All of that out-of-our-control-ness sometimes leads us up the metaphorical garden path where the hopelessness plants and helplessness plants grow so zealously that they block our view – we lose sight of the way forward.

And yet there's such an awful lot that we *do* get to control, get a say in, get a steer on or get to choose.

But, as habitual folk, we might have habits that mean we (not always consciously) relinquish that power stuff to others and feel as though we don't have a say, or perhaps we feel put upon with weighty expectations, trapped in old habits and traditions, stuck in a rut, and have lost sight of a path forward.

But the path is there, it's just shrouded in all the things that loom larger. The things that fog up, crop up, take over, create stress or cause hesitancy, and with the effort of battling all of that comes an energetic and mental toll, a sense that we're not enough, not capable, don't have enough spoons.

We must recharge and then slowly set about making the

changes that are within our control, and the very best bit about that is that once we get going we don't half *get going*, because the momentum of relentless action (of the smallest micro-actions even) isn't half a force to be reckoned with.

Don't put up, shut up and live the life that someone else has decided that you should live. Replace those shoulds with coulds and just feel how you seem to grow a few centimetres taller with the sudden possibility about what you could and *could not* do.

You should XYZ becomes you *could* XYZ, and that little pivot right there gives you options and choices and get-outs and room to breathe.

Clear the path of shoulds and expectations and the over-zealous things that block it with tools and elbow grease and helpers, find a way to hurdle over them, carve another path or completely change direction. It's completely your call.

Don't put up,
shut up and live the
life that someone
else has decided that
you should live.

What are you willing to *not* do?

We're a bunch of dreamers because our brains are wired that way. The brain's endless fantastical imagining helps us solve problems, create new things and believe that things can and will get better. But it can also be a potent source of frustration.

Those dreams of ours, they feel lofty and unimaginable, even though we're the ones that imagined them. The gentle or not-so-gentle diversion and call of interest whenever anything dream-related pops into our awareness serves to remind us time and time again of what we want and of what we're not doing to get what we want.

We know that to get a different outcome we need to act, think and be different, but that can feel nothing short of intimidating. The unknown always does.

But think about it for a minute: this dream of yours isn't unknown. In fact, the picture of it in your mind is clear – it is crisp and it is real.

Perhaps it's not always about 'doing' something new; maybe it's about what we're willing to *not* do.

Become hyper-aware of the choices you make.

You want to be a writer? Think about what you can become willing to *not* do to make time for the crafting of sentences.

You want to create an online store to sell your beautiful crafts? Then perhaps you're going to become willing to *not* make another thing until you've logged into Etsy, Shopify, etc. and created the bones of a store for yourself.

We all have choices, but there are options that support what we're hankering after – happiness, a new job, a dream, a goal – and there are options that don't. Simples.

So . . . what are you willing to *not* do so that your magical and mystical imagination becomes less of a frustration?

Believe you can

We all have these things called 'limiting beliefs', which means you have them and those around you have them too. They're completely normal, completely overcomable, but until we overcome them, they can't half box us in.

Years ago, it was believed that to run a mile in less than four minutes was impossible. But there was a man, and perhaps importantly, a man *and* a team, who totally believed it to be possible. That man was Roger Bannister, and once he had broken the four-minute record in 1954, many followed suit. He believed he could and that he would. And so did those around him.

Gotta repeat that: *so did those around him.*

There's a documentary called *Kim Swims*. It's about this incredible open-water swimmer called Kimberley Chambers who swam a record 48 kilometres off the coast of San Francisco in 2015. She was the first woman to do so and at some point others (if they haven't already) will follow suit. She believed she could and that she would. And so did those around her.

So did those around her.

Limiting beliefs are those thoughts that are attached to something we'd quite like to do:

- *I'm not clever/rich/thin/connected/young/old enough*
- *Maybe one day*
- *I'd love to do XYZ, but I don't think I ever could*
- *I'm too busy*
- *I don't deserve it*
- *I'll fail*
- *Things like that don't happen to people like me*

Remember, not only do we all have beliefs of these kinds at times – everybody around us does too. They come from when our confidence has been knocked, when we've encountered pain, scrapes and obstacles, when we haven't been nurtured, or if we have been, how we've been nurtured or natured.

Unboxing ourselves from our own limiting beliefs is an act of choosing ourselves – our hopes, our dreams, our happiness and our potential. A mighty act of self-care if ever there was one.

But we can't do that work for the people around us, that's on them. What we can do is take note. Take note of the people around us who might find our dreams a bit, well, dreamy. And be careful that we don't let them deflate us, box us in. We can take note of the people who will shake their pom-poms, cheer us on, hold our hands, support us, inflate us and believe that we're possible.

We can take note, too, of the things we say when people share their dreams with us; are we going to be an inflator or a deflator? And that applies to people we know in real life and the people we hang out with online.

It'll be our actions, our resetting of the bar, our stepping outside our own limiting beliefs, that will inspire. Just like it did for Roger. And just like it has for Kim. You totally are that person too.

Don't let yourself be boxed in – you have got this, a squa-dillion times over.

Unboxing ourselves from our own limiting beliefs is an act of choosing ourselves – **our hopes, our dreams, our happiness and our potential.**

8

Words for the days when relationships feel hard

If you're navigating uncertain relationship-related waters and you need a helping hand, look no further. Here are some words laden with understanding, and ideas to get you thinking about it all a little differently.

Life isn't black and white

Well, sometimes it is. But, more often than not it's a rainbow-strobe-lighted-kaleidoscope of differing perspectives, opinions, experiences and circumstances. Because, as people, we are complex beings with a whole heap of adulting stuff to contend with.

And that's tricky, because that's what all our relationships are based on – an ever-changing, undulating combination of those things with infinite possible outcomes and complexities with curveballs aplenty. Is it any wonder then that relationships can be so befuddling?

Life is a mosh pit. It's full of differences and greyness and miscommunication. It's full of assumptions and lemons and emotions. It's full of differing personalities and opportunities and knowledge.

That's why relationships can be the most rewarding yet mind-boggling, bewildering and oftentimes painful things. That's why communication is *everything*; we simply cannot guess what someone else is thinking when the very act of thinking about what someone else might be thinking comes from cognitive pathways strengthened by our unique perspectives, opinions, experiences and circumstances. That sounds like a tongue-twister, and it's most definitely a mind-bender. But we just don't know what's truly going on for other people, even those we're closest to, unless we let them in and they let us in.

We can guess. Oh yes, we can guess. But when we guess we make room for *our* insecurities, *our* emotions, *our* past, and those things dictate what *our* viewpoint of any given situation becomes. When we hazard a guess, it's riddled with assumptions, and you know what the saying is? To assume makes an ass out of you and me. We tend to assume so darn incorrectly that we tie ourselves up in tumultuous knots. We've all been there in the dark of the night, playing out how a conversation *might* go – we even fill in the parts of the people we're having said 'imaginary' conversation with, and it never tends to end well for us.

We can't guess what another person's needs, wants or disgruntles might be, just as they can't guess ours. Communication will always, always, be the linchpin that matters. Without fair, kind and compassionate communication we open the door for assumptions galore, and that's messy. We end up with more questions than answers and more resentment than contentment.

Communication allows room for life to become a team sport; it builds bridges, gives others the opportunity to have your back, it negates the guesswork, helps us to work together and it obliterates the relationship uncertainty that we could all do without, as the world is rife with enough uncertainty as it is.

Don't be afraid to voice what's important to you, and don't be afraid to listen with an open heart and an open mind to what's important to another. If in doubt, talk it out.

Relationships aren't meant to be transactional

If someone does or says something nice for or to you, do you have a knee-jerk reaction to return it? Perhaps you get caught in the volley of compliment ping-pong, unable to receive but, by golly, more than willing to give all the niceties. Maybe someone does something kind for you and, rather than soak it up and feel grateful, you feel a compulsion to hop to doing something kind or kinder back. Or is it all working the other way around with someone in your life?

The thing is, relationships aren't transactional in that way. When people give the gift of their generous words, time and energy, or do something from the kindness of their hearts – it ought to be because they have chosen to freely. Not because they feel they have to because of some perceived external expectation that that's what they should do. And it definitely oughtn't to be just because they feel indebted and need to repay that in some way.

We've all experienced such transactional relationships and they aren't half muddy in the imbalance, confusion and uncertainty of it all. If anything, true trust can't exist in that landscape – the foundations on which trust is built can't be conditional.

If you're only receiving love, respect and kindness on the basis of what you can give or do for someone, or how useful you could be to them in the future, then there's some boundary-shifting work to be done.

Equally, if you only feel as though you're worthy of love, respect and kindness when you're being useful, then there's some self-worth work needed.

You are worthy of love, respect and kindness. End of sentence.

You're worthy because you're a human being. Not for what you might or could humanly do.

What are you putting up with?

They say it's the straw that breaks the camel's back, and so many of us can relate to that: the complete ambush of emotion about something that would feel minuscule in isolation. The onslaught of frustration over something that ordinarily wouldn't make us flutter an eyelash.

And that heavy weight of an annoyance that typically wouldn't register. The 'straws'.

The reason the 'straws' are the thing to crush us is often because we're putting up with a lot of different stuff that they're compounding.

Layer upon layer upon layer of stuff that we've put up with. Those aches, pains and niggles that we haven't made appointments for. Perhaps lousy behaviour from others has become the 'norm'. All the times we've prioritised other people's 'yeses', leaving no room for our own. Holey, fraying, chipped, taped-together slippers/glasses/mugs/pyjamas.

These things can make us feel lost, as though we're not sure who we really are any more.

We put up with these things because sometimes fear looms large. Because our brains don't like change (they're wired to like what's familiar), and so the known becomes more comfortable than the unknown. Because asserting our boundaries can be exhausting, and we're already tired, thank you very much. Because we don't feel worthy.

And so we put it all off until the straw breaks us. Maybe not for long, but we all know when it's happened as there's a sense that we might have blown something out of proportion.

But, if anything, we've done the complete opposite.

Our reaction to those 'straws', isn't a reaction to just those 'straws'; it's a build-up of emotion relating to the whole she-bang. Just a delayed reaction to it. The pain point.

The trouble is, when we get to that point it can be overwhelming to have all those things we've put up with looming over us. It feels as though ev-ery-thing needs action/dealing with/a conversation about/upgrading.

It's too much. It's frightening. It makes us want to hide in a blanket fort.

Can you think of something relatively small that you're putting up with? Something that you could do/address/change in the coming days so that your actions speak louder than those pesky thoughts that tell you you're undeserving, unworthy, a pain in the butt?

Because you're none of those things. You deserve better than the things you're putting up with (and that's a promise).

And you might not believe it yet, which is why we can

choose the tiniest thing, the micro-actions, the not-too-intimidating thing to do.

Maybe it's making that doctor's appointment to talk about what's niggling away in your head. Sometimes it's brushing the knots out of our hair. Perhaps it's taking a deep breath and starting that conversation that's well past its due date. Take a couple of minutes to think of a micro-action you can do right now – go do it!

It's a two-way street

Life is about give *and* take, right? We've all heard that before. Perhaps we've heard it so many times that it feels clichéd and the meaning has washed over us. But it's simple science: cause and effect, opposite and equal reactions.

We can apply it to all our relationships because we can't be all about the giving, nor all about the taking; it's a two-way street – there's reciprocity.

But not always, right?!

There are times when we don't honour who we are and we wrap it up in nobility and generosity. Life throws up situations and circumstances where it can take courage to assert our boundaries and identities. The societal 'norms', the familial, unspoken way things have always been, the want to be liked, the fear of being deemed offensive, the hesitation that comes with challenging something. Those things can make it hard to honour ourselves.

What we do instead is we bend, merge, mesh, compromise and toe the line. We don't say what we mean and mean what we say, so that we can pave the way for a quieter day. We compromise ourselves to make things easier on others.

On the face of it, it seems kind and selfless, but what happens when this takes place again and again and again is that we begin to lose a sense of ourselves. In our bid to be selfless we become self-less.

The kindest thing we can do for ourselves, and those around us, is to honour who we are. To honour our likes, dislikes, wants, needs and identity. To remain unbuckled to the peer pressure, to communicate clearly and honestly, and to no longer apologise for needing things to roll a bit differently from now on.

When we find the assumptions and expectations that people hold of us stifling, we don't have to let them dictate our actions.

If we don't like mashed potato, we don't have to eat it.
If we feel like a mug, we can tighten the ship and change our minds.
When our eyelids are heavy and our bones weary, we can rest up.
When we're asked to do something we don't want to do, we can utilise our 'no'.
When we have an idea that's outside the box, question who said there was a box in the first place.
Wish you could spend Christmas Day in your pyjamas? Do it.

It's not selfish to find a clearly communicated compromise that allows everyone health and happiness and a sense of self. And that includes you. How are you (without necessarily realising that you're doing it) conspiring with others to pave the way for their needs and to make their lives rip-roaring easy, all the while needing more and wanting more and deserving more? For as much as you love, adore and care for others, and support them in honouring themselves – it's a two-way street.

Look for approval within

Seeking the approval of others typically comes from a place where we've at some point been starved of the love and attention that we need. So we learned patterns of behaviour that meant we became proficient at this people-pleasing malarkey.

Most of the time, despite that, we didn't get the praise, approval, love and attention we were after, through absolutely no fault of our own. That's the crux of it. The people who should care for us, love us conditionally, keep us safe and nurture us, shouldn't be withholding any of that vital love, attention and kindness stuff. It's on them, not you. It's absolutely not your fault, nor is it because you have any faults that you didn't receive that stuff. You are not faulty, unlovable, unworthy goods. No siree. Heck no. The complete opposite is true. Honestly.

Continuing this people-pleasing quest doesn't half make a rod for our backs. It means we're constantly on high alert looking for any opportunity to dive in and be of service, to help, to make someone smile, to do good, to ease their pain. And we get royally good at it too, so much so that we can't feel good about ourselves unless someone else is feeling good about us. That's the slap-in-the-face bit, the bit that hurts and leaves us feeling empty quite often. If someone shows any sign of being even a smidgen unhappy with us or the world, then that awful berating self-chatter starts up and irreverently highlights the coulda, shoulda, wouldas. We hop into action to try to make things better, no matter whether we've done anything wrong in the first place, no matter whether it's our place to do so, no matter what. It makes for a wonky distribution of power in all our relationships.

The only thing that really matters is that you approve of you. And if you don't, start making the decisions and choices and actions that will help you get there. Compromising who you are to keep others happy means that slowly, bit by bit, the essence of you will diminish, and that would be a crying shame, because you (who you truly deep down are) are important, worthy of happiness, valued, needed, enough.

Shower yourself with the attention, love, kindness, praise and approval that you're thirsty for, and make space to relearn, reparent yourself and to discover who you are, without those people-pleasing rods for your back.

Compromising who
you are to keep others
happy means that slowly,
bit by bit, **the essence
of you will diminish,**
and that would be a
crying shame.

There's got to be some give and take

We're well versed in the nobility of giving. Of the karma, the good feelings, that being generous can evoke. Giving can be transformative to both the giver and the givee.

But there are many of us who keep trying to give when we're running on empty, not considering for one jot that there's a karma carnival waiting to give back what we've given; the love, care, space and generosity.

You see, giving is applaudable. It's a nice thing to do; it helps those in need and without it the world would get more topsy-turvy a lot more quickly.

It's when we're not in a position to give, yet keep trying to give, that *our* worlds get topsy-turvy. And we're not talking about physical or monetary giving here; we're talking time, energy, hope, encouragement, emotional support and head-space – those things aren't a mystical resource that magically replenishes as we give, just as physical and monetary resources aren't. If only.

Those resources require topping back up, and to do that we need to get comfortable with taking what we need. The trouble with that is that taking has all kinds of negative connotations. We don't want to be 'takers' or seen as 'takers' because in our minds it sounds so wrong. So selfish. So self-indulgent.

There's an equal and opposite reaction to every action we take. Where there's giving, there must be some taking. Where there's taking, there must be some giving.

Consider the joy we experience when we help someone, when we give to them. In blocking that giving to us, aren't we then blocking the joy we've experienced? Heck yes.

It's one of those reframe thingamabobs. When we consider that we're a burden, unworthy and just hate asking for help, consider it this way instead: we're opening the channels to let the joy of giving flow both ways.

You need an 'out' too

People who have experienced acute pain from trouble and strife tend to be phenomenal listeners, because they wouldn't wish their darkest times on anyone. If there's anything at all that they can do to help another, you can bet your bottom dollar that they'll show up.

And the power of the knowing nod that comes from really listening and being listened to is immense. It's like a soothing balm to the soul, this kindness malarkey.

If you're one of those mighty good listeners, though, who is listening to you? Do you have people who see and hear you? Where are your outlets, stress-busting, fear-expressing, being-heard stuff coming from? Because you need them too; we all do.

If you're always taking in the worries, strains and stresses of another and you're their go-to for someone to sit with in the darkness, then the biggest of thank-yous to you – we need more of you in the world and you probably don't realise just what a massive difference you make to the hope and lives of those around you. All the thank-yous and then some. Buuuuut – and you knew this was coming – right?

All that taking in needs an 'out'. There needs to be a support network for you. You can't give, give, give at the detriment to your energetic, emotional and mental health. It's safe and OK to take sometimes. Whether that be to find yourself some 'listeners'; to find a way to vent your not-so-nice stuff; journal, exercise, create, blog, join a support group, punch a pillow – anything to remove and express the stuff that's taking up headspace and weighing you down. Because you are very important too and, as much as it's amazing that you're so giving and kind (it *really* is), there's enough for you too. Give to you, be kind to you – we don't want the darkness to come and bite you on the bum again anytime soon.

If you're one
of those mighty
good listeners,
who is listening
to you?

Blooming conditions

In order to bloom, different plants need different climates, food, conditions. There will be some plants that bloom to the detriment of other plants. There are some plants that are a bit tricky and need a little more attention. There are shade-loving, sun-loving, water-loving, dry-climate-loving, hardy, perennial, annual, all sorts of plants that all come with instructions when you buy them from a garden centre. There are programmes aplenty on how to nurture these plants, because getting the conditions just right for them is a reward in itself.

And that's true for you too. When you assert boundaries, prioritise self-care and change your conditions to ones where you can bloom, that's a reward in itself.

So, when other people make you feel bad for blooming, remember those plants and how fastidious we have to be to get those conditions right, and stop to wonder why other people are so opposed to you getting your conditions just right for you.

Unfortunately we don't come with instructions about our perfect climes; we've got to go down the try-it-and-test-it route, but in doing so it doesn't matter if other people think we're a bit awkward or 'off' for asserting a boundary that works for us. It doesn't matter if we're considered temperamental or demanding for asking for what we need. It doesn't matter if someone thinks we're 'cold' because we're pulling back from a situation, an environment or a relationship which is toxic for us. *They don't get to bloom at the detriment of you.* Nuh-uh.

You, with no ifs and no buts, deserve to bloom.

Empathy as rocket fuel

There are times when we so dearly want to offer comfort that we stumble over the words.

There are times when the suffering of others takes our breath away and we just don't know what to do or say.

There are times we reach out for help to be met with awkward silences that feel like rejection.

There are times when 'I'm fine' covers a multi-layered complexity of pain and anguish that we can't quite put into words.

There are times when we compose a text message and agonise over getting the tone right, so much so that we end up not sending it at all.

And there are times when we're right in the middle of a conflict or a disagreement and the words stumble out, but they're words of frustration and anger, laden with ego and judgement and wrong-footedness.

We place a great deal of responsibility on our words; they have the power to hurt and to soothe, to humiliate and to reassure, to belittle and to empower.

But there's this thing called empathy that is like rocket fuel for our relationships. Empathy cements connection; it enables us to see life from a different perspective – it helps us to sit with another's pain and it takes the emphasis away from the words and the fixing, and places them on feelings instead.

Empathy is the tool that allows us to imagine what experiences might be like for another; it helps us delve into situations we've not experienced and to gain an understanding of what it could possibly be like.

When the words can't quite come, when we get tongue-tied and have so much to say but aren't sure how to say it in a way that's useful, helpful and hopeful, we can take a breath and dive head first into empathy.

Don't be afraid to ask questions.
Your willingness to sit with someone through the darkness is precious.
Sometimes our actions speak louder than our words.
Words that come from a place of empathy are the 'right' words.
Try not to give unsolicited advice.
Empower, encourage and empathise.

Supporting someone through tough times isn't ever easy; seeing things from another person's perspective is a skill to hone, and we sometimes put ourselves under undeniable pressure to get things oh-so-perfectly-right for fear of making a situation worse. The very fact that we care, that we're trying and that we're doing our best, is *everything*.

Empathy enables us to see life from a different **perspective** – it helps us to sit with another's **pain** and it takes the emphasis away from the words and the fixing, and places them on **feelings** instead.

9

Words for the days when you're being unkind to yourself

If you find that you're giving yourself a hard time of it, this chapter is crammed full of soothing and empowering words to help you turn that around.

It's OK

It mightn't always feel it, but . . .

It's OK to change your mind.

It's OK to draw people in.

It's OK to hold some people at arm's length.

It's OK to soak up the silence.

It's OK to want more rambunctiousness.

It's OK to address the sources of stress.

It's OK to talk about the hard things.

It's OK to not feel ready to talk about the hard things.

It's OK to write a letter if saying the words is too difficult.

It's OK to be honest even if it's not what someone is going to want to hear.

It's OK to like what you like.

It's OK to not feel guilty about everything.

It's OK to assert yourself (there's a difference between assertion and aggression).

It's OK to make time for the things that make your heart feel full.

It's OK to spend much less time with the people or on the

things that make your heart feel like lead.

It's OK to delete, mute, block.

It's OK to disagree.

It's OK if others disagree with you.

It's OK to lean into the warm people.

It's OK to give and receive second chances.

It's OK to politely decline unsolicited advice.

It's OK to make the appointment and use the helplines.

It's OK if people don't understand your decisions, as long as you do.

It's OK to stay in your pyjamas today.

It's OK to remove yourself from situations that aren't healthy for you.

It's OK to always, always, always do life your way.

In a world that sends us messages about being kind and then isn't always kind to us when we do what's kind for us: remember that it's your life – nobody else's – and it's your responsibility to make sure you enjoy it as best you can. And equally, it's not on you to split yourself into a squadillion pieces to compromise yourself, to try to make other people happy – that's on them, that's their responsibility. Boundaries, boundaries, boundaries.

Bump yourself up

Life, per se, doesn't revolve around you. But *your* life absolutely does. You're right at the epicentre of it. Smack-bang right in the middle. Your decisions, your actions, your choices, everything you think, do, are, impacts you.

But if we were to look at your mammoth to-do list, I'm hazarding a guess that it doesn't at all revolve around you. Not in the slightest. Perhaps you don't even feature in it.

The tasks, the chores, the dizzying stuff to get done, it's most likely life admin that serves you on some admin-y, need-to-pay-the-bills-and-have-food-on-the-table level. But the core of you that has wishes and dreams and wants and needs and whimsical thoughts of what you'll do when life lets up – that part of you is probably nowhere to be seen on this 'ere longer-than-the-equator to-do list of yours.

Yes, we know, it comes rife with connotations of selfishness and indulgence and all the 'I just don't have the time's. For the record then: it's not selfish, it's not indulgent and you do have the time.

For one day or two (or however many you fancy) make a record of where your time goes – where you spend those twenty-four hours of your day. Include sleep, work, study, responsibilities, social media usage, Netflix – pop it all in. Laying it out means that you can renegotiate some of the slices of your day for you. And if you can't, you're going to need to think about what you can eliminate, automate or ask for help with.

Because you matter.

Let your actions speak louder than those words. Bump yourself up your own to-do list. Go on, insert a line between the 'this's and 'that's and put something in there that's just for you.

Now then, if you've never done this before your heart might race at the novelty of it, at what feels audacious and loaded with 'Can I really do this?' *Yes, you can.*

And the best bit about it? You'll get used to it – your days will be peppered with things that you find joy in, people around you will learn from you and be inspired by you, and if you have children, take warmth in the fact that what they see you do is what they grow up thinking is normal. It's true there may be people who have resistance to it at first, but that's probably because to bump you up you might need to bump down some of their requests for your time and energy – but they can bump themselves up their own lists instead of always relying on you. So, if they grow up seeing you burn yourself out to keep those around you tip-top, that's what they're likely to grow into. And you want more for them than that, surely? You want more than that for you too.

Be who you want to be

For a lot of us, from the moment we're born people look for clues as to who we seem most like. Do we have Grandad's nose, Grandma's auburn hair, or perhaps our eyes are the same colour as Mum's?

As we grow older those comparisons mushroom to who our personality traits, habits, likes and dislikes remind everyone around us of. These are not always dished out in the most complimentary of ways either: 'Grrr, you are *just* like your blimmin' [insert whoever they're finding unfavourable here]' or 'You remind me of Ferris Bueller and not in a good way.'

It can leave us feeling diluted, as though we're a patchwork of a person, as though we're not always sure of who we are.

You may well have inherited physical attributes, learned or imitated behaviours, and now call sideburns 'sideboards', because that's what your parents told you they were called and it stuck.

But what you are is you – a person in your own right – and how you view yourself is waaayyyy more important than the uninvited observations from your nearest and maybe not so dearest.

You're not just like every Tom, Sharon and Barry; you are unique, and in most non-gene ways whoever you choose *you* want to be.

> *We get to reinvent ourselves over and over and over as we*
>   *roll through life.*
> *We get to shake off identities and stroll into new ones.*
> *We get to decide who we are and who we are not.*
> *We get to decide how our days and ways will play out.*

You're you, and that's exactly who you're meant to be.

Please choose your happiness

Happiness often feels like a glimmering, glistening and glittering mirage far away in the distance, completely inaccessible, unreachable and unattainable.

In fact, happiness is agonisingly within reach for each and every one of us. It's not some 'when I do this, I'll be happy' thing. It's like bad moods and bad times – it passes, but is within reach if we'd only reach for it. It's not the destination either; it's not something that's full of conditions and only happens once XYZ has been completed/nailed/achieved – it's right there at our fingertips at all times.

The thing about happiness is that we often feel unworthy of it because of some ickiness we're carrying: shame about something, guilt about something, self-dislike for some reason. And so we block the things that make us feel delicious and joyful, making those dark days become dark weeks and so on.

Happiness lies in the things that feel delicious and joyful. It's quite often that simple: bare feet in grass, that first hot drink of the day, listening to music that lifts you up, spending time with people who are infectiously kind and funny, crisp clean sheets, that gorgeous scented candle, losing yourself in a book, watching funny videos on YouTube, wave-jumping, sand beneath your toes, soft fluffy slippers, ice lollies on a hot day, receiving a random act of kindness, being the giver of a random act of kindness, working towards a future that lights you up like a Christmas tree, jumping on a trampoline or bouncy castle, playing board games, watching a film, using that 'for best' crockery, dancing in the rain, colouring in, the smell of essential oils, and so on and so on.

As kids we gravitate towards the things we love to do, the things that make us smile and laugh loudly. Give yourself permission to sprinkle your days with all that's delicious and joyful to you, whatever that might be. Schedule them in, if you like. Those things might become the glimmer of the light in the heavy darkness; they might shine out of the darkness and give you a reprieve, if only for a spell. They'll pass because everything does, even the darkness – that's why consciously choosing the deliciousness gives happiness better odds.

Please choose you – the happy, funny, kind, courageous, fun, playful, joyful and intelligent person that you are. You are all those things and so much more. The dark times have just done a right royal job of convincing you that the opposite is true and it's a right royal fibber. Please choose your happiness and health.

Two opposing things can be true

Two seemingly opposing things can be true at the same time: the rain can fall and the sun can shine, and together they create a rainbow.

We might be right-handed but we can still write with our left hand (albeit not so practised and neat).

We can be in the deepest, darkest depths of depression and experience a spontaneous bout of laughter as something out of the blue strikes us as funny.

We can look forward to something yet dread aspects of it.

We can be incredibly educated and in the know on certain topics/subjects, and ignorant and oblivious to others.

We can cry with laughter and we can cry with pain.

And, where you're concerned, there will be imperfections – because we all have them – but there will be a riot of blimmin' brilliance about you at the same time. We all have strengths and weaknesses; it's the accepting and acknowledging and not getting too attached to either or neither that we find tricky.

Only owning our weaknesses and casting a shadow over our brilliance ignores the very duality of who we are. And that duality is important because just as we oughtn't to be defined by our brilliance, we oughtn't to be defined by our imperfections either. We're so much more than those things. Always.

Allow both to co-exist, knowing that in doing so you're neither solely imperfect nor solely perfect – there's a rainbow of character that's created when both exist at the same time. And that's a beautiful thing. We often love the quirks of others because they're what makes them, them. Fall in love with yours too.

We all have strengths and weaknesses; it's the accepting and acknowledging and not getting too attached to either or neither that we find tricky.

Confidence can be rebuilt

It *is* a hard-knock life. It really, truly is.

Problems never go away; they just change shape and size.

There are so many ways that can knock us down and usually we're really quite good at getting back up again. Even if it's a teetering climb with a helping hand or two.

These relentless knocks, which are part and parcel of life, aren't all equal. There are some that we've dealt with so often that they're like water off a duck's back. There are some that floor us for a spell, but once we've gathered ourselves we can dizzily get back up on to our feet. And there are those awful ones that erode away at our confidence until we feel stunned into inaction, doubting all our skills, experience, abilities, everything about our existence.

Confidence isn't a static thing. We're not just confident or not; we waver depending on the situation, person or the events leading up to now. It is all relative.

If, though, we've had a barrage of really hard knocks, then our confidence may well have dwindled so badly that we end up procrasti-tweeting, procrasti-gramming, procrasti-cleaning, procrasti-painting, procrasti-napping, procrasti-anything that we feel will come easily-ish to us so that we don't have to address the colossal imbalance of confidence for whatever's the next thing that we have to face.

Here's the thing about confidence, though. We often wait for it to gallantly arrive before we do whatever it is we feel unconfident about. Confidence can be rebuilt, no matter how bad the knocks have been, but it always takes determined action (which on the realllllllly rough days will have to wait until we have the spoons).

Confidence can be rebuilt in baby steps by testing the waters in a space you feel a little wary and hesitant to occupy but really want to. It can be rebuilt by doing the thing you thought you could not do. It can also be rebuilt by inhaling as much knowledge as possible. It can be rebuilt with practice. It can be rebuilt by reminding ourselves of all the times we did something we didn't think we could do. It can be rebuilt by limiting the time we spend with people who belittle, criticise or pooh-pooh our dreams. And it can be rebuilt by finding mentors and guides who will walk the path with us. It can always be rebuilt; it just takes time.

If you've experienced knock after knock after knock after knock, and you feel worn down and worn out, always rest and recuperate first. Give yourself space to catch your breath before you attempt to get back up. Because get back up you will. Remember: you're down but not out, never out. And when you're ready, and you feel that feistiness return in dribs and drabs, start taking steps to rebuild block by block, step by step.

Confidence can be rebuilt, no matter how bad the knocks.

Don't apologise for who you are

OK, hands up if you catch yourself saying 'sorry' more times than you care to mention?

Slowly raises hand

You know the times:

Sorry (when someone stands on your foot).
Sorry for the delay in replying to an email.
Sorry to interrupt you.
Sorry we've run out of milk.

And so on and so on and so on it goes.

Do we really feel regret when someone has stood on *our* foot? When we live with other grown-ups, is making sure we always have milk really just on us? Are we expressing sympathy that we've chosen to focus on other things and not been living in our inbox or sitting waiting by our phones for a message to pop up?

We become so used to being sorry that we're on the tip of apologising for our very existence. Our knee-jerk constant over-apologising is laying so much blame, shame and responsibility at our doors for the things that are out of our control, such as making someone cross – but how they react to our behaviour is on them, not us.

In doing so we're undermining our confidence, self-esteem and identity, and evading as much awkwardness as possible. Expressing sympathy or making amends when we've done something wrong has become a way to dodge the discomfort or be amenable. But there's something in feeling discomfort – it's honest. It's honest in a way that uttering a willy-nilly 'sorry' when we don't at all mean it, not in the way the word is designed to be used, isn't.

When we refuse to shoulder the blame for something that wasn't ever our fault in the first place, we're creating something honest. We're asserting boundaries. We're stepping into self-worth, shoulders up, head raised, and we're saying no to shame and guilt that never belonged at our doors in the first place.

Try to be mindful of the sorrys you're giving away. Pause and consider if you've really done anything wrong in the first place. Pause and ask yourself if you really are sorry. Pause and decide to not diminish the value of who you are by needlessly throwing those sorrys around.

Are you hiding your light under a bushel?

Don't be bossy, they said. Let so-and-so have a go, they said. You're such a chatterbox, they said. Stop being so sensitive, they said. Stop showing off, they said.

In other words, don't be too this or too that. Conform, comply, hide your light under a bushel. And so we do.

We dilute, we toe the line, we stop taking up space and we hide – not in the sense that we camp out in some cave in the wilderness, but we gradually dull the things that make us, well . . . us. The things that come easily to us. The things that make us shine.

In the short term it feels easier to live this way, less friction-ed, less annoying for those around us, less against the grain.

But in the long term we end up making choices we wouldn't have made. We end up living a life that wasn't intentionally what we would have lived. We end up compromised. We end up being like everyone else.

Whatever it is that makes you, you, is what the world needs more of. Your quirks, your you-isms, your eccentricity, your natural talents, your abilities, your 'you'.

If you're reading this and thinking 'I don't have any of those, I'm not talented, I have no abilities, I have no me-isms, I have no eccentricities, no me-ness', in the kindest possible way you're wrong. You have those in abundance, but you've got so exceptionally good at hiding them and toning them down that they're hidden from you now.

The criticisms and judgements we've heard repeatedly throughout our lives are often where our magic lies. 'Bossy' kids are usually budding leaders. Children who want to give everything a go are children who are motivated, enthusiastic and courageous. Young people who talk a lot tend to have a fantastic grasp of language and great social skills. Sensitivity in kids shows an understanding of emotion, self-awareness and empathy. Kids that 'show off' tend to be comfortable in their own skin and confident in their abilities. Such magic qualities.

That magic, though, makes other people uncomfortable because they either have a different kind of magic and they're playing that unhealthy comparison game, or perhaps they're trying to make other people around you feel better by dampening your magic.

What's so frustrating and sad about that is that you begin to believe that those magical parts of you should be shut down, that they're not magical, but it's not your job to make other people feel comfortable in who they are. It never was and never will be.

Your magic makes other people **uncomfortable** because they either have a different kind of magic or they're playing that unhealthy comparison game.

You're a champ

It's not the awards, public recognition and accolades that make a champion a champion. It's all the stuff that goes unseen, un-rewarded, unnoticed and un-shouted from the rooftops.

It's the stuff that's done regularly with deep breaths and sometimes through gritted teeth: the bouncing back up, the eff-ort, the practising, the rehearsing, the learning to fill the gaps in our knowledge, taking the tough life lessons on the chin, the lifting up of others, the deliberate routine tweaking, the mind-ful decision-making, the self-care, the doing our best, the sweat, the tears, the wobbles, the stretching of our skills, the stepping outside our comfort zones and the asserting of boundaries.

The true measure of strength isn't the bulging of biceps and grimacing roar; it's how we react in the moments we feel at our weakest, and there's evidence aplenty that says you're one strong cookie. You've got through all those horrendous hours, the ones that you didn't think you'd get through. You've con-tinued to put one foot in front of the other even when the view has been foggy and bleak. When hope has evaded you, you've created more. You've dug deep and found grit that surprised even yourself.

Because nobody is including you in some honours list or presenting you with an award in front of an applauding audience or popping an Olympic medal around your neck, let's take an appreciation break to applaud *you*.

You have champ qualities in abundance, and then some.

Don't forget to build in the rest and recovery, though – all this champing needs it.

10

Words for the days when life is wearing you down

When you feel depleted and bedraggled
and as though the well of you has run dry,
dip gently into these words and take
what you need from them.

Give yourself all the time you need

At some point in our lives we all experience a pivotal shifting of the axis of our existence; when someone we care about dies, when we become parents or struggle to become parents, when there's prolonged conflict or estrangement, while enduring long periods of ill health, if we've experienced trauma, anything really, that's knocked our socks off and rigorously rocked the boat.

These things change us, and they change the way we view the world around us. We don't feel the same as we once did, and in those times we may feel unanchored, as though we're not as sure of our self-identity.

It's during these times that we might feel as though we're living in a parallel universe, going through the motions, emotions haywire, and the smile on our face mightn't be quite as sincere as we'd like.

We need to let go of the self-criticism and self-judgement of not being who we might have been.

When the axis of our world is rocked and we're changed from that, it takes time for us to heal, for the dust to settle, for us to become used to this post-shape-shifting version of ourselves. Until that happens and we've a more certain view of who we are after all of that, then we will very much be putting one step in front of the other just to get through.

If you're in the middle of this, please don't worry and put yourself under undue pressure if you change your mind about things a gazillion times over, if you can't face certain situations or people, if you need space to feel whatever it is you're feeling, if you need professional help, if you feel cranky and grizzly, if you need a chance to understand yourself better, if you need time to mourn that pre-whatever-it-was version of yourself, if you need to explore who you are in the here and now, if you wear fake smiles because you don't yet have the words you need to express yourself.

It all takes time – give yourself all the time you need.

People don't need fixing

When we care incredibly deeply about people, we can sometimes take on things that aren't ours to take on. Their pain, their problems, their anger, their responsibilities. We take it on as though it's our own and make ourselves responsible for things that really aren't ours to do so.

It comes from the loveliest of places, this 'taking on' malarkey. A place of kindness, compassion, vulnerability and empathy. But empathy isn't at all about taking things on. It's about the ability to understand how somebody else might feel. What empathy isn't is being engulfed in *their* stuff.

When we dive into the problems of others, we tend to don our capes and do whatever's within our power to extinguish their discomfort and pain. In doing so we often wish that someone would swoop in and save us too.

The trouble with all this, however, is that it's an infringement of boundaries. An almighty one.

You see, boundaries are the space between us all, the healthy space that grants us room to breathe, negotiate expectations and sets what we are (and aren't) responsible for. And the one thing we're not responsible for is the happiness of others, just as they're not responsible for ours.

When we have the urge to fix other people, it comes from something that needs fixing from within us. When we tie our happiness to that of another, we're blurring the boundary lines.

There's a massive difference between caring deeply for someone, sitting with someone in the darkness, holding space for them and offering advice when asked for it, or swooping in with unsolicited advice and taking over and fixing stuff. Our way mightn't be the right way for them and vice versa. Our problem-solving skills, self-helpfulness and life-navigational skills atrophy when they're not used regularly. When we shoulder responsibilities that are not ours to shoulder, we're stealing that opportunity for growth, self-fulfilment and sense of accomplishment from another.

Chances are we've got obstacles, issues, wonky things of our own to deal with. Adding on layers of other people's stuff drowns out *our* stuff, the stuff that might be holding us back and causing us night-time worries.

It comes from the kindest and noblest of places, always, but that doesn't mean it's the kindest and noblest of things to do.

When we shoulder **responsibilities** that are not ours to shoulder, we're stealing that **opportunity for growth, self-fulfilment** and **sense of accomplishment from another**.

You're not 'needy' for having needs

Each and every one of us has needs, there's no disputing that. According to Maslow's Hierarchy of Needs, our universal needs include: physiological needs, safety needs, belongingness and love needs, esteem needs and self-actualisation needs.

That's quite a broad spectrum of needs. Keeping those needs met and topped up can be a rigmarole and then some, one rife with decisions, life chaos, circumstances, postcode lotteries, cultures, change and conflicting demands on our time and energy and finances and attention.

At any one time we might have a need, or multiple needs, that isn't being met. Needing. In need of. *Needy*.

This 'needy' word is bandied about as though it's something shameful and is used to describe the words and actions of someone 'less than'. It's often accompanied by that same sneer or eye-roll used when calling someone out for being 'attention-seeking'. And that's got to stop.

Being in need isn't a cause for derision. Not from any angle you want to look at it. It's a signal for action, encouragement, support and change. It's also not something to be ashamed of or to feel guilty about.

Just as attention seeking is often care seeking, being needy is expressing one's needs.

And that's a cause for applause.

Life wouldn't half be less of a kerfuffle if we all felt comfortable communicating our needs. We could do away with the treading on eggshells, the 'I'm fine's, the inability to take what people say at face value, the worrying and the wondering. Because *we'd know*.

For some reason, talking about our needs makes some people uncomfortable – typically those outdated stiff-upper-lip types who'd rather we buttoned up and shut up – but even they have needs too.

You have every right in the world to tell people what you need and that your needs aren't being met. Needy simply means in need. It's not a dirty word. It's how things are for you right now. You, as a person, are not less than for having needs – we all have them. You are not a problem or the problem. Arguably the people who have a problem with you expressing how you feel and what you need are a huge part of the problem. Not you, though, OK?

Put some self-care anchors in place

Life can get all Groundhog Day-y and the days mesh and merge and intertwine with non-stop things to do, places to be and people to see. And in among all that we're supposed to self-care it right up. It's a hard balance to find, particularly if our self-care requires chunks of time – the one thing we feel is in short supply.

The thing about self-care, though, is it really isn't *just* about massages, heading to the beach and pampering. For sure those things can be self-care but more often than not it's the simpler things that comfort, reassure, declutter and ground us. The anchors.

These are the things we've hopefully scattered through-out our day to help bring us back in touch with ourselves. The things that create a pause from the daily grind and give us a chance to top up our energy. The things we do that tomorrow-you will thank now-you for. The things that help us optimise our psychological and physical health.

Now then, these anchors will vary from person to person, but have a think and have a go at identifying yours. Grab a pen and some paper and make a list of those comforting, reassuring, decluttering and grounding things that work for you. Then sprinkle them, like confetti, throughout your day – whatever the day holds. Give yourself the frequent chance to touch base and recentre and enjoy a spot of self-care and self-kindness.

Here are some ideas if you need help getting started:

Read before bed for an hour
Take your lunch break away from your desk
Open and sort your post
Walk barefoot on the grass
Meditate
Make lists
Express the stress
Check in with the people you like and love
Have enough water to drink
Set some boundaries
Budget
Take your meds
Stretch your legs
Breathe in fresh air
Pet a pet
Cuddle someone or something
Peruse photos that bring back good memories
Step towards a dream

Our lists will differ, but the idea behind these self-care anchors is that we identify and thread them throughout every day. That way we're consistently and persistently topping ourselves up. These things are important and need to be woven in with all our other daily tasks.

Address the proverbial 'grit'

Grit in our shoes can be annoying but not quite annoying enough that we always get rid of it as soon as we notice it. It can even hurt a little as it rubs, but not always enough for us to stop what we're doing and remove it.

We keep on keeping on. We adjust for it. But we're mindful of its existence at every step we take and it's a mighty relief once it's gone.

We've all got a bit of grit like that in our lives: something that's a nuisance, which perhaps causes us some low-level mental pain or stress, gives rise to tension and is at the back of our minds more often than we care to admit.

The 'if only's, the 'I must remember to's, the gnawing of resentment or perhaps anger, and the 'I really need to's.

We all have life-grit, something that's not so painful or annoying that we *have* to attend to it immediately, something that we're putting up with, which if dealt with would make us feel better, as though a weight had been lifted.

Perhaps it's a conversation we're putting off, aches and pains we need to address, some post we need to open, a parcel we need to return, a boundary we want to straighten –

whatever it is, it's there and we know it's there, and for some reason we carry it with us mentally every day rather than sort it out or ask for help with it.

Dealing with those life-grit things is an act of self-care because future-you will thank now-you for handling it.

The wear and tear

We all have 'em – those days when nothing seems to go right; we bang our toes, hear bad news, make clumsy mistakes, feel prickly, irritated and beaten, and things go wrong every which way.

The wear and tear of that squiffiness is palpable; we feel it in our bones, in our overzealous thoughts, in the circumstances around us, and in a lowlights reel that feels longer than the equator. We feel mentally and physically done in.

That wretchedness that we feel sometimes, or oftentimes, tends to be because we're all out of alignment with something. Perhaps in who we're being, of the things we're saying, of what our actions are, where we're working, of who we spend our time with or how our days play out. The squiffiness feels so awful, but it contains an awful lot of wisdom too, if we look and listen and learn, and take action to realign our misaligned bits.

There are times where we're so misaligned with where we thought we were heading, of what we'd hoped for ourselves, that it feels like an almighty battle that's beyond us. Remember, though, there's nothing that's beyond you.

There's no obstacle, problem or rubbishy issue that you can't overcome, because you're more magical, capable, courageous, kind, clever and valued than you could ever possibly imagine. But when we look at all the crummy things in their entirety, it's easy to feel overshadowed by them, to feel stuck and to feel small.

Pay heed to when you feel awful and look at those times with an inquisitive eye: what were you doing, what had you done, who were you with, what were you thinking, what had you consumed (food, drink, media, entertainment), where were you?

Then also pay heed to the times you feel so unsquiffy that time seems to zoom by: what were you doing, what had you done, who were you with, what were you thinking, what had you consumed (food, drink, media, entertainment), where were you?

When the lousy stuff is overbearing, overwhelming and overcooked, believe that you have what it takes to get yourself through it – because you do. Learn too from the unlousy stuff; notice what you're doing and who you're with when you feel good, make tiny steps every day to realign who you are – what you say, who you want to be and what you do – with that vision you had for yourself. It's all still possible; *you're* still possible.

There are times where we're so **misaligned** with where we thought we were heading, of what we'd hoped for ourselves, that it feels like an almighty battle that's beyond us. Remember, though, there's **nothing that's beyond you.**

Is it loving you back?

Sometimes we pour ourselves into something and we're left feeling unfulfilled and exhausted and resentful.

Whatever that 'something' is – a person, a project, our work – it hasn't loved us back if it's left us feeling a little bit broken.

For if it had, we'd surely feel proud, stand taller and feel accomplished. Even if we felt tired and in need of a break.

It's a test for whether something tops us up and simultaneously nurtures us as we nurture it – this marker of how we feel before, during and after.

Other things, though, we give our all to and, despite the need to recharge, we still have a beaming smile on our face. A sense that it was worth the effort. Those things? They've loved us back.

Ultimately there are things we feel nervous about but, once done, we feel as though we're walking on sunshine, and there are other things we rush towards with open arms only to be left feeling down in the dumps. We can almost pre-empt the answer to the question 'Will this love me back?' by pondering how we'll feel after it's done.

That presentation at school or work? The thought of standing on a stage with hundreds of sets of eyes looking at you might fill you with dread. But how might you feel once you've shared your important message? Hyped up? Proud? Amazed at yourself that you did it? It's going to love you back.

Your job? Fast-forward to five years from now. How does future-you feel after five years of commitment, dedication and slog? If you feel resentful, angry that you're still working there and nauseous at the very thought, it's not loving you back.

Not everything has to love us back, and not everything will, but it's important to make sure our lives are sprinkled with some things that do.

Embrace your childishness

When we're little, we don't half wish our lives away as we grow impatient for more independence and autonomy. When I'm eighteen, I'm going to [insert goal here].

When we're much older, we don't half wish we could relinquish the responsibilities and weights on our shoulders (a teensy break would do) that perhaps, if we were lucky enough, we didn't have to bear as a child.

There's an odd middle ground, too, where being childish becomes an insult, a slur, that we cast around when someone doesn't appear to be mature enough, adult enough, for our liking.

Perhaps we're a little too quick to cast aside those childish perspectives we might've once had, that others might've once had: the curiosity, the awe, the barrels of laughter, the cheekiness, the imagination, the magic that we could find or make willy-nilly.

You see, so many of us adults are living lives without curiosity, without awe, without barrels of laughter, without a dose of cheekiness, with little imagination. And if we believe that we no longer have the capacity for those things, we're oh-so wrong.

All those things – if we can dig deep for them, stoke them and make time for them – are the kind of joyous self-care that not only feels pretty darn good but which creates long-lasting memories. That magic is within you still – even after all this time – but it's all around you too. That double rainbow, the gentle sway of snowflakes, the glistening frost on the ground, birds frolicking in the park, the stars as they twinkle, hearing someone laugh so uninhibitedly or the sun as it rises and sets.

In the trickier times when we get swept away with expectations or tough stuff then we need to make our own joy and reconnect with our inner child, choose to view the world through the lens of curiosity and awe, and rekindle some of the dreams we had when we were younger.

There is joy to be found, always. Sometimes we think it's turned its back on us but typically we've turned our back or shut our eyes to it. Go find it. Embrace your childishness.

What's on your magical things list?

Sometimes our lives don't half feel like a drag. The monotony, the endless grey, the life admin, the hurdles, the problem-solving and so on. It wears us down and wears us out.

But now, everyone's starting to wonder about ways we might break the cycle of all that. After all, they say, a change is as good as a rest.

It's worth sometimes looking at life from a different angle, wondering how we can make sure our days are sprinkled with things that encourage us to shake free the dust, to pause, to breathe, to be still and to smile, so that the drag isn't the continual hamster-wheel-norm of what we do and, therefore, how we feel.

You see, us folk, we're habitual, and that can serve us well in lots of cases and be quite comforting, but in lots of other ways it can make us feel stuck, bored and helpless. We can lose our sense of selves in the demands, the loudness and the higgledy-piggledy nature of life.

Your challenge, should you wish to accept it, is to gradually make a mega-mega list. A list of the:

- *Things that made you smile, feel comforted and laugh with joy as a child.*
- *Activities you'd get so lost in as a child that it was bedtime before you knew it.*
- *Tried and tested ways of feeling comforted and reassured.*
- *Favourites: drinks, snacks, music, films, books, smells, colours, people, crockery, flowers, clothes, blankets, etc.*
- *Times you felt calm, at peace, recharged.*
- *Things that light you up and energise you.*
- *Self-care stuff that you've always wanted to give a go, as well as the things you do but would like to do more often.*

And with your magical things list, you're going to schedule it into your days. You're going to endeavour to go for a walk and smell the freshly cut grass or emerging flowers, if that's on your list. You might take a flask of your favourite hot drink and your book and sit outdoors for ten minutes. You might splice up the most mundane of tasks with a 'song break', a slice of your favourite cake, some windmill arms or some Lego playing. Whatever floats your boat, whatever brings you joy, makes you smile, makes things feel a little lighter, whatever it is that's made it to your list and no matter how seemingly small those things are, use them to signal a reset and new micro-beginning throughout your day.

The pleasure really is in simple things. Harness them. Scatter your days with them to make your days that little bit brighter.

A **change** is
as good as
a rest.

Changing the lens

When we've had a really rotten time of it, we often look back through a lens of frustration, greyness, loss, impatience or anger.

Frustration that things didn't unfold as we'd have liked.
Greyness because once you've known the pain of truly tough times it can tinge all times.
Loss because sometimes we lose parts of ourselves to the darkness or we lose time.
Impatience because we're not where we'd hoped we'd be.
Anger that this has happened at all.

But it is possible to change the lens that we look through to reflect. *It is.*

Where there is frustration, there could also be pride that we got through even when we doubted that we ever could. We displayed a strength and courageousness that we didn't know existed within us.

Where there is greyness, there could also be a pink hue cast on all the people and things that pulled us through and provided comfort in the most uncomfortable of times.

Where there is loss, there's also often gain: lessons, under-standing, coping tools, compassion, empathy, rediscovery, shackles shaken off, a realisation that we can't ever know what lies ahead so we might as well embrace the gift of the present moment, prioritise the things that do light us up, and follow those dreams of ours because 'impossible' can be shifted to 'I'm possible' with a little space and grace.

Where there is impatience, there's also an eye opening that life isn't ever linear – not for anyone, despite how often it looks that way from the outside. Life is rich with peaks and troughs; it has forks in the road and crossroads, and there's darkness and there's light. There's tweaking, pivoting and flexing. There are choices and there are options and there's an endless possibility, even for us. Even now. *More so* now because we know we can overcome the hardest of hurdles. Even if we need a break first to soothe our battle-worn-ness.

Where there is anger, there's often change: self-care rou-tines, boundary setting and shifting, trying new things, a shimmy out of the confines of societal, cultural and relatio-nal expectations. Anger can evolve into the bottled energy of enthusiasm to propel us to where we want to go, be and do.

The fact you got through the tough stuff shows gumption, tenacity and a dig-deepness. The fact that when the chips were down you didn't stay down, shows that there's hope inside you that can't be extinguished *no matter what*. The fact that when you didn't think you had what it took to get through you found it, shows an inner badassery that will one day, when you've space to reflect through a different lens, astound *even you*. You're outstanding despite, in spite of, *because* of, what you've gone through.

Worthy, even when . . .

You are worthy of all that's good.

Worthy of love
Worthy of happiness
Worthy of help
Worthy of kindness
Worthy of acceptance
Worthy of that nap
Worthy of using your 'best' dinner set
Worthy of socks without holes
Worthy of the last biscuit
Worthy of that hug you need
Worthy of appreciation

And there are no 'buts' about it. You are worthy of all that's
good, even when:

You make a mistake
Change your mind
Say no

Trip up
Question yourself
Question your reflection
Your brain is being a sod
Other people are being sods
You're being a sod
Life weighs heavy
You carry regret
You feel unworthy

Worthy, worthy, worthy, worthy, worthy – that's what you are.

11

Words for the days when you're in the murky thick of it

If the term 'treading in treacle' resonates
with how you feel right now and you're dealing
with problems left, right and centre, there's
quietude and fortitude to be found in
the words that follow.

Rock. Hard place

Think positive, they say. Step back and look at the bigger picture. Do some yoga. Do more of this, less of that. Try this, try that.

When we're in the heavy, fog-laden, leaden-limbed thick of it, we feel superglued stuck, depleted, despondent, frustrated and alone.

Well-meaning advice can feel cumbersome because, nine times out of ten, it's action-orientated. The problem with that? It makes us feel as though we're not doing enough, and quite often we're here because we've been doing and giving 'too' much of ourselves away.

When we're all out of fricks to give and peeling ourselves from our bedsheets takes it all out of us, action-based stuff feels nigh on impossible. And then that rotten, hopeless, damaging guilt-comparison loop is fed again. I 'should', I 'ought', it worked for 'Shirley' and 'Rob' and 'Gandalf'. These thoughts are monsters we have to slay by the second.

And that's rough. And tough. Some days take it all out of us just to get *through* the day. The action-orientated stuff being a reach too far.

It's the getting from here to *there* that we can't quite figure out, that we're blind to when we're constantly having to slay bullying dragon-esque thoughts. Rock. Hard place.

But the things that help us aren't always action-orientated. Sometimes it's a matter of giving up the thoughts that are wrong for us, instead of creating new behaviours, which will create the headspace, emotion and energy that you need to do the things you deem right for you.

Feel free, with wild abandon, to give in or give up the things that don't serve you. Here's a list of ideas to get you started:

This false illusion of perfection.
The futility of juggling all balls perfectly in sync.
Of being like anyone other than who you are.
Give in and accept the help that's offered.
Your body's pleas for rest.
Give up that 'life is linear' timetable of milestones that you set yourself.
Trying to please everybody.
Giving away your yeses.
Trying to be all the things to all the people.
Putting yourself down.

Feel free, with wild abandon, to give in or give up the things that don't serve you.

Embrace all of you

We're complex, we're layered and we're full of parallels and opposites.

There's laughter and there's pain. Joy co-exists with heavy baggage. Mistakes and growth are intermingled. Life can be sweet and sour, bitter and salty. All at the same, somewhat confusing, time.

There is no absolute to life, no black and white – we exist in a multitude of shades of grey. Whatever we're feeling isn't the be-all and end-all of who we are – we're far more complicated, interesting and varied than that.

The thing about the tricky times is that no matter how large they loom, you loom so much larger. There is always so much more to you than any lemon life might throw your way. That's why we can simultaneously be sad about something and excited by something else. It's how we carry the grey but still shine so brightly. It's why the bad times don't in any way diminish our beauty, but instead add a depth that might not have existed before, a place where there's a heightened empathy, passion and kindness.

When the tricky towers over you, please know there's more

to you than that and that there's more good stuff to come. Having depression, tough times, dark thoughts – those horrible things we might experience – they don't define you, they don't make *you* horrible. You've so much more to you than those times. Those tricky times, they do pass and there will be brighter days and brighter ways.

If the bad times are the waves crashing to the shore, then you are the sea. If the sad times are like lingering grey clouds, then you are the sky. If the dark times feel like mud, then you are the mighty oak.

You are full of heart and grit and strength and variety, and you are important and valued. You are so much more than what life throws at you.

You're not a let-down

When we mentally get proper wonky-tonk, we know about it because it's increasingly difficult to function; our cognitive abilities slow down or ultra speed up, life feels insurmountable and we don't always recognise the person that looks back at us from the mirror.

Before we get there, though, there are many, many cues, signals and early-warning signs that say 'slow down', this doesn't seem kind to you, you need a break, you're compromising yourself and so on before our minds and body slam on the brakes.

Those early-warning signs will differ for us all, as our 'norm' will vary, but they can look/feel like:

Extreme lethargy
Tiredness that no amount of sleep will cure
Confusion
Unusual aches and pains
*Inability to think straight and solve problems that would
    once have been a walk in the park*
Withdrawing from friends and family

Cranky with lower tolerance than normal
Clumsiness
Appetite changes
Feeling overloaded
Experiencing decision fatigue
Catching every cold and bug going
Tearful
Wanting to run away

Some of these things creep up on us and some sway us about a bit, but very often they don't halt us in our tracks in the way that our mind and body need them to.

If you're not feeling OK, it's all right to make changes, to move appointments and meetings around, to take mental health days, to promote self-care to the top of your list, to heed those signs before they floor you, to not get lost in the noise. That health and happiness of yours is important. It's not always about what you can do for others; it's also about what you can do for you.

It's OK to cry

It's OK to cry when we're happy or sad. It's OK to cry when we're feeling angry-mad or when we're feeling bad. It's OK to cry whatever the weather and it's OK to cry whenever we can't hold it all together. It's OK to cry when we're little or old and it's OK to cry even if none of this is what we've been told. It doesn't matter who we are or what we do as a job, it's still OK to have a big almighty sob.

But crying doesn't always *feel* OK. Crying can feel painful; it can look messy and it can sound primal. It's the most natural way of expressing stuff that there ever was. We did it instinctively as babies until someone filtered us with their words, their expressions, their inability to provide comfort, the shushing, the 'don't cry', the 'please stop crying's.

But keeping all that stuff in? That's never going to end up well for us. 'Better out than in' sounds trite but it's tritely true. When we internalise all the stuff that makes us cry, we're not giving it an out, we're not exploring it, we're not expressing it and we're often not growing through it.

And it doesn't have to be a mighty shower-cry or a pull-up-the-duvet-over-our-heads-and-let-rip-with-tears kinda cry.

Emitting our emotions can take on many forms: journalling, talking, singing, punching a punchbag, letting out a giant scream, pounding the ground as we walk, doing something creative. There's a reason why we often feel better when we've done any of those things; it untangles the tangled, it expresses the stress, it gives energy to the emotions, it de-stresses our muscles and it makes space for us to feel something, anything, else.

It really is OK to cry. Sometimes we have to wade through the awkward awful stuff to find calmer climes.

When we **internalise** all
the stuff that makes us cry
we're not giving it an out,
we're not **exploring** it,
we're not **expressing** it
and we're often not
growing through it.

Don't let the pain be in vain

The great and glorious emotions of joy, peace, pride and love are the ones we wish we could catch and bottle up. And then there are the emotions that feel so yucky that they make us want to run for the hills: guilt, anger, pain.

These emotions of ours are our natural automatic responses to something that's going on for us, whether that's internal or external.

When we do something, we try to ascertain what emotion we'll experience and when we'll experience it. Emotions are often a precursor to a change in our physiology or a change in our behaviours; if we experience happiness, it motivates us to jump for joy, to spread a beaming smile across our face and to lean into it, to do more of whatever it was that created that emotion in us.

Pain is mightily useful if we've broken our leg – it alerts us to the need for help, for medical attention, and when we're in recovery it tells us if we've overdone it and need to rest.

Mental pain is no different, not really. It's alerting us to something that needs our attention, something we may or may not need support with, and it tells us if we've overdone it and need to rest.

There's an instinct to ignore the mental wound, but we wouldn't ignore a physical one in the same way, especially if it got infected and started going green. Mental wounds, when unattended to, continue to cause us pain until we take stock of them, and it's always in our interest, as it would be with any physical pain, to do so sooner rather than later.

Don't let the pain be in vain. Pause to find out what's causing it, what's not working for you, and take congruous action or seek appropriate care. In the same way you would if you had a splinter. Future-you will thank you for it.

Accept help

Needing help isn't ever going to be a comfortable place to be whatever the circumstances. It means we've run out of or are very close to running out of spoons, answers, ideas, energy, hope. Feeling vulnerable can be frightening, painful and dark. If we sit in that place for too long and don't ask for help when we need it, it'll beat us. Asking for help doesn't make us weak; in fact, it's a tool for us to try to take back the reins – it can be empowering and it'll probably be the best thing you've ever done.

Ask for help waaaay before you're at the jacking-it-all-in stage, *please*. Ask for help even when your hope is dwindling at a rate faster than knots. There is hope even when you can't see it or feel it. Everything is figure-out-able even when you've run out of ideas and ways to figure it out. You can and will get through whatever it is you're facing with the right help and support. We don't have to face things alone. There are people who have been where you are who have enough experience, hope, energy, ideas and things to lift you when you're in need.

There is **hope** even when you can't **see** it or **feel** it.

Under pressure

We all deal with pressure in different ways; some of us thrive, while others flail. Our pressure points – the point at which the pressure we're under becomes too heavy to bear and something has to give – vary, but we all have them.

And it's usually our health or our essence that becomes compromised. We're not infallible. We can only take so much.

Sometimes the striving gets in the way of our thriving.
Sometimes we take on so much that our back aches
and stoops.
Sometimes we try to be all of the things to all of the people.
Sometimes we get lost in the lists.
Sometimes asserting our boundaries is exhausting.
Sometimes change and growth hurt.
Sometimes we're just spent, empty and splutter to a halt.
Sometimes loneliness can knock the wind from our sails.
Sometimes our emotions are emotioned out.
Sometimes the weight of the painful stuff buckles us to
our knees.
Sometimes we're blind to the next step to take.

We get to the point where we feel lost, in acute pain, full of despair and as though we don't have what it takes to deal with anything. But don't ever think that's weakness.

It's the stress fractures of carrying a load for too long. It's not that we're delicate; it's that we've been so strong for so long and, by golly, we just need a rest. A chance to take stock. Time to recharge and replenish.

Please take that rest. Please.

We have so much to give, so much. Of that there is no doubt. But to give we need to also take – it's one of those universal life-law things. Take what you need to help you rise up and roar. Take what you need to replenish the depleted. Take what you need so that solutions arise, seemingly out of nowhere. Take all the time there is in the world; life isn't a race. And most importantly, take what you need to feel like you again.

Self-care doesn't have to be expensive

Everywhere we look it seems as though people have got this self-care stuff nailed: the spa days, the holidays, the shopping trips . . . Those are the things we hear about and see.

We might not be able to afford to do those things – financially or energetically.

The thing is, though, as nice as those things might seem, they're not really the epitome of self-care. And it's easy to get confused about what self-care means. It's also easy to see how self-care can become another stick with which we beat ourselves – if that standard is what we're reaching for.

To take care of something we need to care about it, and we don't always like ourselves very much. Self-kindness doesn't always come easy and it's nearly always intolerable when we've had a long period of depression doing all the talking in its loud and cruel way, convincing us that we're worthless, helpless and hopeless.

At its essence self-care is a term for recovery and growth. It's the thoughts, actions and decisions we make – even the really teeny-tiny ones – that help us feel better psychologically, physically, emotionally and socially.

So, while those gorgeous spa days might be self-care for some, when we're running on empty, self-care becomes critical and it takes on a different guise. These things totally and utterly count as self-care too:

- *Sleeping*
- *Changing our mind about something*
- *Asking for help*
- *Turning off our phone notifications*
- *Making an appointment to see the doctor/dentist*
- *Keeping a positivity jar or drawer of the compliments, feedback and kindness we've received*
- *Learning about an illness or ailment*
- *Brushing our teeth*
- *Having a glass of water*
- *Letting help in*

And on the bad days, those things may feel impossible, but be mindful of your breath and rest and do whatever it takes to get through the day. This is self-care too.

Sometimes the seemingly smallest (completely free) acts are the most courageous, triumphant and hugest acts of self-care.

Self-care is the thoughts, actions and decisions we make – even the really teeny-tiny ones – that help us feel better **psychologically, physically, emotionally** and **socially.**

12

Words for the days when it all feels helpless

Of all the chapters I hoped you wouldn't need
it was this one. I'm sorry everything feels bleak
for you. If seeds of hope, possibility and
strengthening are what you're in need
of right now, please read on.

In the eye of the storm

We seek this continual utopian middle-ness in life, where we can gently bob along, feeling zen, feeling oh-so balanced. And we want to be there and stay there for ever.

Yet life is undulating; there's the ebb, the flow, the surge, the retreat, the current, the tides, the storms – there is no middle-ness.

When we're smack-bang in the midst of a terrifying storm and it's blowing a disruptive and destructive gale, it's hard to see past it. It's hard to see anything else because the storm demands our attention; it blunts our view and it drags up everything in its wake, leaving us feeling messy, a little broken and definitely worn out.

If we bide our time, with the right help and support the storm passes, leaving us feeling bedraggled, vulnerable and triumphant. As the dust settles and we embrace the calm, we can experience all the groovy stuff again. But we often don't properly relax into the groovy stuff because we know that the odds are that there's another storm brewing, right?

And we fear the storms because they're so painful, so loud, so damaging, so demoralising. The storms leave a residue that we struggle to shake off, which discolours the calm. We know they won't last for ever – nothing ever does. But isn't that the thing? *Nothing ever does*. Not the calm periods and definitely not the storms. They don't last for ever.

We allow the storms to cast a shadow over the light, but in the same way we could hold on to the light to illuminate the dark. There's nothing as mighty as a glimmer of hope, of believing when we're in the middle of the grot that it *will* pass.

However aggressive the storms you're sitting through right now, you can and will get through them. Probably not alone; we all need hand-holding, support and guidance to find our way through the darkness. Probably not unchanged either – everything we go through alters us and moulds us, and sometimes the storms teach us about changes we can make to ensure that we're more storm-proof in the future: boundaries, self-care, support networks, etc. You *will* be triumphant, you *will* smile again, you *will* belly-laugh again and you *will* experience calm again.

Weather the storms and consider them preparation for the most epic of karma carnivals heading your way; you've been dolloped with the rough stuff, the good is sure to be a-coming.

We allow the storms
to cast a shadow over
the light, but in the
same way we could
hold on to the light to
illuminate the dark.

The Compound Effect

You may, or may not have, heard about the Compound Effect. It's used to iterate how the smallest of decisions, the smallest of savings and the smallest of actions can compound over time with momentum, results and interest in the bestest way possible.

But what about the compound effect of stress? Of worry? Of the niggly little problems?

If all the good things compound into greatness, surely the less good things compound and take their toll too?

They absolutely do. Sustained stress, worrying and problem-solving can strengthen our resilience – to a point. But when there's seemingly no end to it, when it goes on and on and on, and it feels as if life is relentlessly throwing lemons our way, it's going to get exhausting. It's that pressure cooker feeling we experience, as though all that steam has nowhere to go and we feel as though we're going to explode with it all.

And it's all very well urging us to reach out for help, but some of us don't have a 'village', we don't have sturdy support systems, we don't know who or where to go for help, because, honestly, there's nobody really there – there's nobody reaching in either.

That's a lonely, terrifying and painful place to be. Sod being stuck between a rock and a hard place; it's a canyon-esque crevice and it feels insurmountable.

Understandable, then, why we might not manage to pluck out those positive thoughts, why those affirmations can rankle, and those 'speak to your friends and family' posts can highlight all that isn't.

So, what do we do?

We initiate emergency self-care mode – we self-care in the littlest ways and we do so constantly and consistently – even when it feels awkward and alien to do so. Those small acts of self-care compound and gain momentum.

Self-care, when we're stuck in a canyon-esque crevice, is the most uncomfortable and annoying thing because it doesn't feel as though it's getting us anywhere. It doesn't feel as though it's addressing the barrage of problems, let alone solving them. It doesn't feel *enough*. It feels counterproductive and counter-intuitive and that's largely because we've stopped feeling as though we matter. Self-care is an act of care, and when we're in a canyon-esque crevice we've typically stopped caring about ourselves many moons ago.

But care we oughta (and I don't use that word lightly). We are more than this canyon-esque crevice that darkly looms over us – even when we don't feel it. The self-caring, the self-kindness, the patience, the stopping, the nurturing is like weight training for our souls – it's what helps us move mountains, climb out of the crevice and reverse the compound effect of the mud, the pain and the bone-crushing weight of whatever it is we're carrying.

You, as much as anyone in the world, deserve this care. Start here, start small, start now and start with what you've got and who you are within this moment. But start showering yourself with care and love and all the good stuff, because it's that which will help you to recharge and slay the rough stuff.

Problems don't form a queue

Resilience comes from overcoming problems that we might not initially feel able to overcome.

In an ideal world the problems we face would form an orderly queue in size order from smallest to largest. We'd grow more confident and resilient in a nice linear fashion. We'd feel more equipped (hopefully) to deal with the little-bit-larger-than-before problem and we'd be able to focus on one problem at a time. There would be a gentle pause of a breath in between each one too. How blimmin' lovely that would be.

Life, however, has other ideas, and those ideas can be wonderfully, excitingly awesome. But they can also be messy, painful and proper meddling. And when we're in the middle of that gargantuan pile-on, we feel small, we feel powerless and we feel completely and utterly defeated.

A knee-jerk reaction might be to commando roll out from underneath it all and run as far and as fast as we can. But, sadly, these things don't tend to sort themselves out without us.

When life is piling on top of you and you can't see a way through, take a pause – there's always power in the pause, however counterproductive it may feel. Focus on your breathing: breathe out slowly to the count of five, breathe in slowly to the count of five, and repeat until you feel calmer. Once you feel more settled, gather your thoughts and deal with one thing at a time – the 'thing' you deem to be the most urgent 'thing', not the 'thing' that other people are dangling in front of your face to get your attention. Politely ask those people to wait, you'll get to it, you'll get to them, you're doing your best, you're doing something else right now. Because even when we feel powerless, we do still get to make the choices that are best for us.

Even then, don't forget to take a nice gentle pause of breath in between each 'thing'.

Create a horizon

One of the inevitabilities of life is that it will continually and consistently serve up challenges, obstacles and things that topsy-turvy our worlds. But while the gloomy stuff isn't always within our control, we can create a horizon to help us see past it.

If we've always got things peppered ahead of us that we look forward to – things that fill us with excitable butterflies of anticipation, in spades of peace, pockets of fun, an event, a book, a film release, a holiday, a get-together with people who lift us up – then when the rough rolls around, we have something to look past it and see. We can look beyond the curveball and see a time ahead that will give us a reprieve.

If at the start of a new day, a new week, a new month, a new year, a new decade, there's nothing ahead that brings a smile to your lips at the very thought of whatever it is – create it, schedule it, plan it, plot it. Because those things we can control. We can pepper as many of those things into our days as we can shake a whistle at.

They don't have to be big things either: a day trip to the seaside, a walk around a lake, time to reflect away from the riff-raff of family life, a bubble bath after the school run, finding a craft club or meet-up, learning something new, a daily dance break to your favourite tunes, treating yourself to a candle of a much-loved smell, making an extra effort to prepare a delicious lunch, FaceTiming someone you adore, making space on a shelf so your treasured knick-knacks can be on display, reading through cards/emails/letters that were written with love, making a start on that book you want to write, dedicating a block of time to self-care each day (even if it's fifteen minutes), whatever it is that makes you feel expanded at the very thought of it – make a conscious effort to do more of that.

We can't always pre-empt the grotty and, when we're stuck in it, it feels as though that's all there is, but everything that's great can be engineered and put into place. Create a horizon for yourself, so that when you look ahead there's sunshine and rainbows in among the thunderous clouds.

Our thoughts lie

When life has us bogged down with all the crud it could possibly throw our way, it's difficult to remain positive. Even if we're naturally a glass-half-full kinda person, when the obstacles are many, it can be arduous, mentally exhausting and hard to catch a break.

Something else happens at those times too; our thoughts find it hard to remain positive. As if it's not enough that the real world has become tricky, the internal one can too.

When our thoughts tell us that we're unworthy of love, happiness and companionship – they're lying, because everyone is worthy of those things.

When our thoughts tell us that we're a burden – they're lying. Carrying a burden doesn't make us a burden.

When our thoughts tell us that the world would be better off without us – they're lying, because that isn't *ever* the case. *Not ever.*

When our thoughts tell us we're deserving of the tricky times, that we've brought them on ourselves – they're lying. Tricky times will always roll around for everyone, and they'll always roll away again too.

When our thoughts tell us that this is it, it's not going to get any better – they're lying. Everything passes and eases eventually: the good, the bad and the downright painful.

When our thoughts tell us that we're not enough – they're lying. We were born enough.

These lies, though, they hurt. It literally does feel as though we're at war with ourselves, and, unlike everything external, we can't escape our minds – where we go, they go.

The lies are plentiful but they're all, *all*, reframeable because they're complete untruths. Our thoughts are like passing clouds (some bigger, greyer and murkier than the wispy ones); they absolutely aren't fact. *They are not fact.*

Just because we can't see something or imagine something, doesn't mean it's not there.

Just because we can't see or imagine better times, doesn't mean they're not coming.

Just because we can't see or imagine our own greatness, doesn't take away that other people can.

Just because those thoughts feel true, doesn't mean they are.

When our thoughts tell us that the world would be better off without us – they're lying, because that isn't *ever* the case. **Not ever.**

Don't give up before it gets better

When things get really gnarly, don't give up. Give in to the offers of help and support and rest, but don't give up.

The torrid stuff fades away eventually. It always does.

You only need to look a little to see that there are masses and masses of stories of overcoming adversity. Those people are no more special nor more extraordinary nor more equipped than you. *They just didn't give up before it got better.*

They didn't roar out of the doldrums and beat their chest either. They would have wobbled with fear, battled with distrust and wondered if their efforts were in vain. Hope would have been eroded into microscopic rations and the overwhelming feelings would have been of exhaustion, depletion and uneasiness.

Read the stories, watch the films and TED Talks, speak with the people and ask them questions, follow them on social media, and you'll see that it wasn't always a bolster of courage in the way we think of it in superhero terms. Those people were superheroic because they refused to give up, even when every cell in their body screamed at them that they couldn't do it and wouldn't get through it.

Courage isn't a feeling of courageousness. We often do the most courageous things when we're feeling frightened and feel like giving up.

You're a superhero, although you mightn't know it yet. There's nothing, *nothing*, that you can't and won't get through. Please don't give up before it gets better.

Acknowledgements

With hindsight there's a common thread of kindness throughout my life and I'm so utterly grateful for it. Even the not-so-kind people and times are far outweighed by the kind ones.

In reading my acknowledgements in my previous books it's clear to me that all those people I mentioned are full to the brim with kindness, and being on the receiving end of it brings a warmth and comfort. And like a moth to a flame I'm drawn to those people.

I'd like to acknowledge quite a list of people for their kindness. Ready?

My husband, Dom, for his unwavering support, head pats, the thousands of cups of tea, the wiping of tears, the holding of hands, the hot-water bottles, kind words of encouragement, his relentless cheering and for always believing in me. The list of his kindness is enough to fill a book!

Our daughter, Peggy, who is so kind that when she found a slow-worm nest in the garden she made sure they had a plentiful supply of weeds to eat at the entrance. There's a long list of things like this, including the time she rubbed my forehead when I told her I had a poorly brain (depression), the countless cards and pieces of art I find on my desk, her beautiful insights and capacity for love, and the way she cares for our dog as though he's her baby.

My beautiful Mother Hubbard, who instilled kindness into my sister and me with her words and more importantly her actions. It blows me away how she celebrates and champions us all and makes sure there's never any doubt that we're loved. And loved hard. It makes me cry thinking about all the gazillion ways she's shown kindness.

My younger sister, Clairie, is as kind as they come, and when she cares she goes all in, full throttle, and I've been so lucky to grow up and grow older with her.

My hilarious dad, who is so much kinder than he'd want you to know (and now you all know – sorry, Dad, but it's all true!).

There's so many more people I want to honour with a paragraph of their own but I fear I'd end up writing a book just on that, so in no way less kind are these lovely lot:

Ryan, Livvy, Rosie, Auntie Ammy, Uncle Keithie, Wendy, Adgie, Paul, Teresa, Holly, Zach, Tom, Pam, Rach, Rob, Sienna, Sofia, Lou, Sam, Amy Trevaskus, Caroline French, Tracy Hayne, Kate Penhale, Karen Lang, Tambo Lemon Meringo, McHuggus, Stephbeam, Naomipops, Imogen, Tina Bernstein, Rosie Johnson, Jemma Thompson, Fiona Dermott, Raegon Guest, Emma Gannon, Emma Preator, Mrs Bradley, Rich and Caroline Mehta, and so many more.

Without the kindness and generosity and dedication this group of powerhouses possess there wouldn't be any books, let alone this one, so to Abbie Greaves, Olivia Morris, Katie Greenstreet, Ru Merritt, Paul Stark and Lucinda McNeil – all the thank-yous, unending gratitude and appreciation, and then some!

About the author

Jayne Hardy is the founder and CEO of the Blurt Foundation – a social enterprise dedicated to helping those affected by depression. The Blurt Foundation's website received over 1.2 million unique visitors in 2019 and their Self-Care Starter Kit has been downloaded over 15,000 times. She has spoken and written about her own experiences of depression and self-care on BBC Radio 2, at TEDxBrum and in publications and websites such as the Huffington Post, *Grazia* and Virgin.com, to name a few.

Her innovative use of the internet to bring about positive social change was recognised when she won the TalkTalk Digital Hero Award in 2011 and in 2014 she was included in *Marketing Magazine*'s list of Top Ten Digital Mavericks. Jayne has been mentioned as one of the nineteen inspirational women leading the way in mental health by Rethink as part of their International Women's Day celebrations, and in 2016 Jayne led the viral #whatyoudontsee social media campaign.

Jayne lives in Cornwall with her husband, their daughter and their dog.